# the creative retreat

*everything you need to create
your own personal retreat*

## Jennie Moraitis

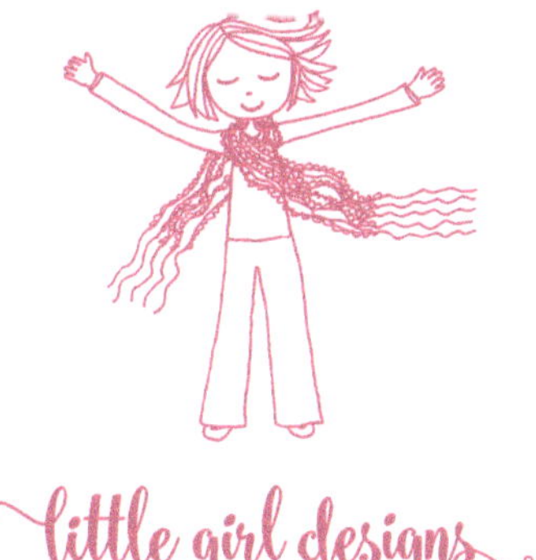

*little girl designs*

## Copyright & Permissions



ISBN-13: 978-0-692-71360-0

Edited by Ashley Brooks, www.brookseditorial.com
Designed by Tim Moraitis, www.moraitisdesign.com

Little Girl Designs
PO Box 243
Beaverton, Oregon 97075-0243

www.littlegirldesigns.com
www.makearetreat.com

*For my sweetheart, who believed in this
project from the start — I love you.*

*And to our precious daughter, who always
has a song in her heart and is the
sweetest gift we could have ever asked for.
We love you!*

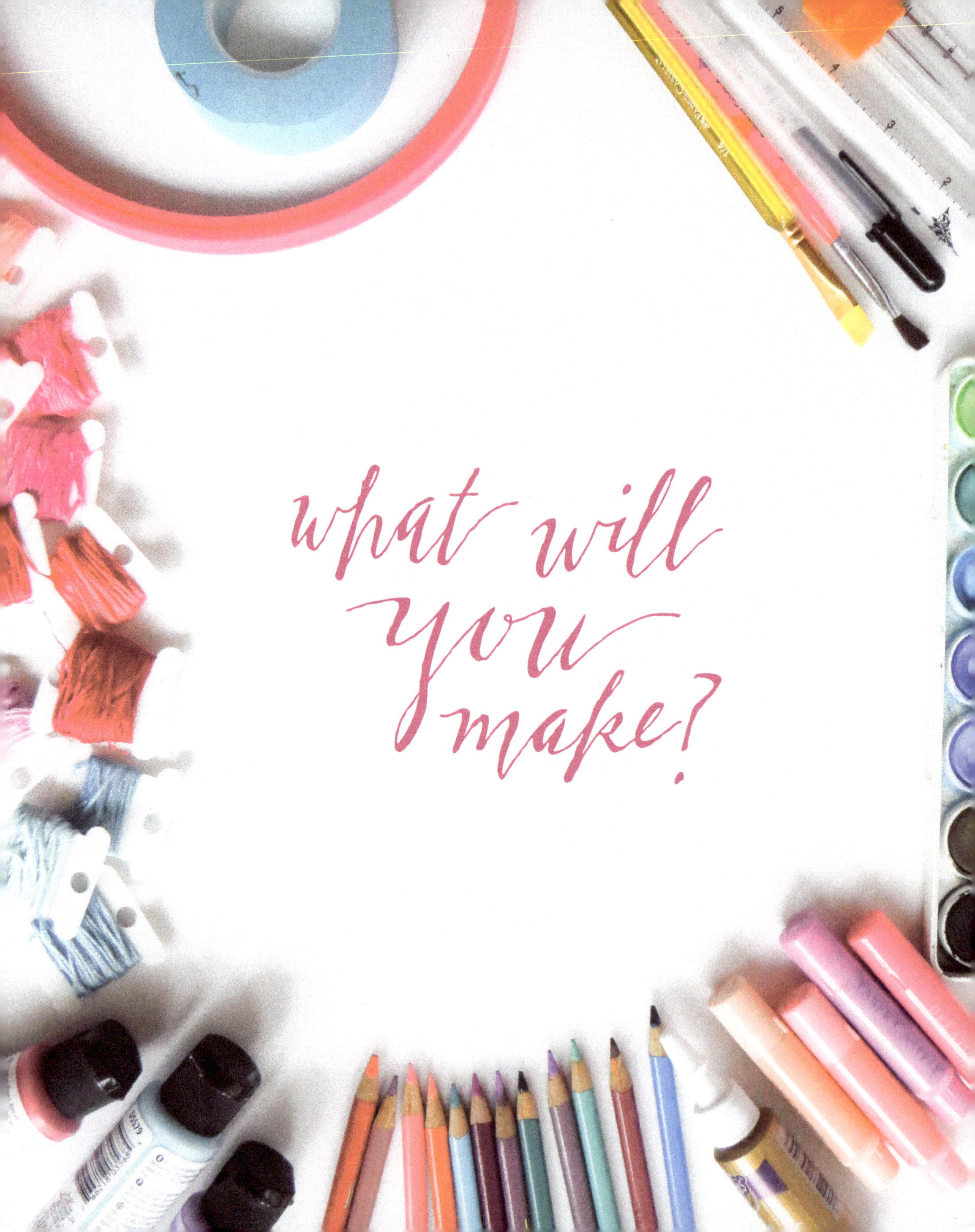
what will you make?

# Contents

# introduction

If you're like me, the idea of getting away for a creative retreat sounds like heaven. Staying in rustic-luxe cabins, conversations with new friends, delicious food, and FINALLY, time to work on our creative projects.

Years ago, I was introduced to the idea of a creative retreat like this. I didn't have the finances to go at the time, but that's when I made a decision. I decided to make my own creative retreat. Armed with my bag bursting with journals and pens, I drove to Manhattan Beach in Los Angeles one Saturday morning. I drove straight to my favorite bookstore and gathered several creative-project books. Stack in hand, I sat down and started my retreat. Okay, I probably also had a coffee and a cookie nearby—you know, for sustenance.

It wasn't long before my heart was singing. Forget the rustic resort! This was what I had needed. Seeing such beautiful art and reading about each person's process was enough to get me back into my groove. I put the books back and headed outside to the cafe chairs to write in my journal. I doodled, made lists, prayed, and sipped

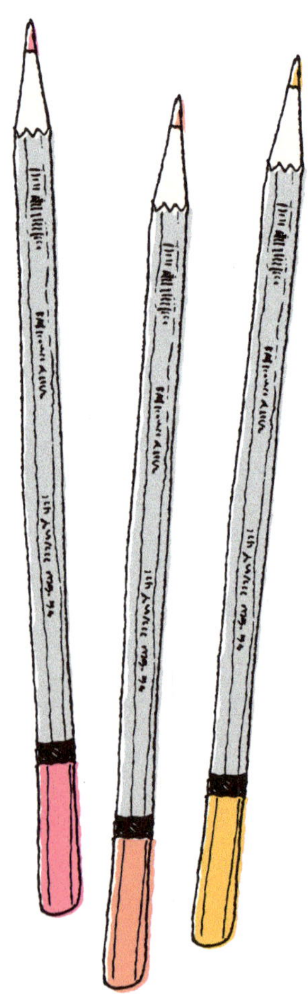

coffee. This. Was. Fun. The words began to slow on
the page, so I packed my bag and drove over
to the ocean. Walking along the sand with the waves
building and crashing next to me filled my soul
to the brim. It was time to go home.

Not all of my retreats followed that formula, but
they all had the same purpose: to nourish my
creative spirit on a regular basis. Through the years,
the retreats have morphed into my daily
routine, so I find I'm taking micro-retreats almost
every day. They're the cup of tea and a bit of
reading at naptime. Painting in the morning before
anyone's up. Drawing with my daughter. It has all
made for one richly creative experience.

I don't have all the answers, but I have discovered
you can grow your creative practice bit by
bit over the years without setting aside gigantic
chunks of time.

I'm so glad you decided to join me on
this adventure.

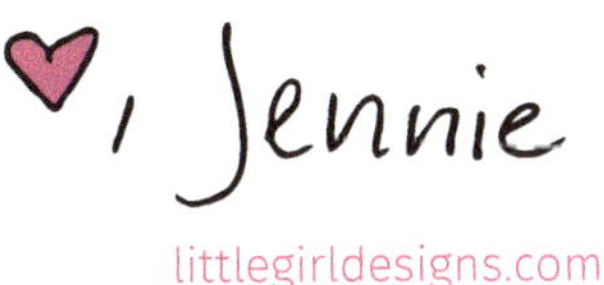

♥, Jennie

littlegirldesigns.com

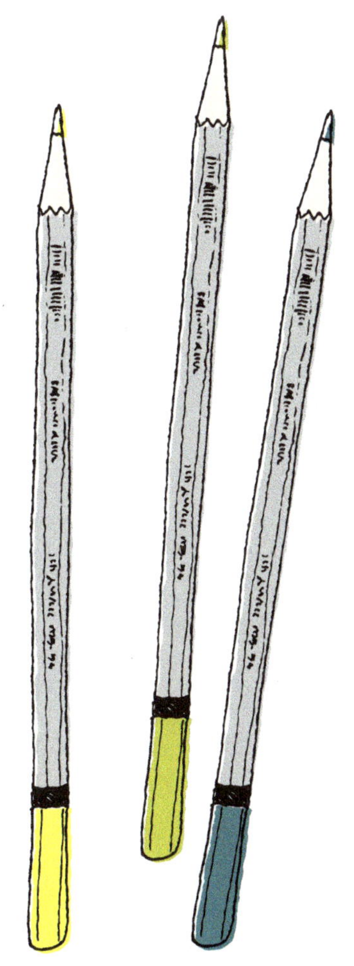

# getting started

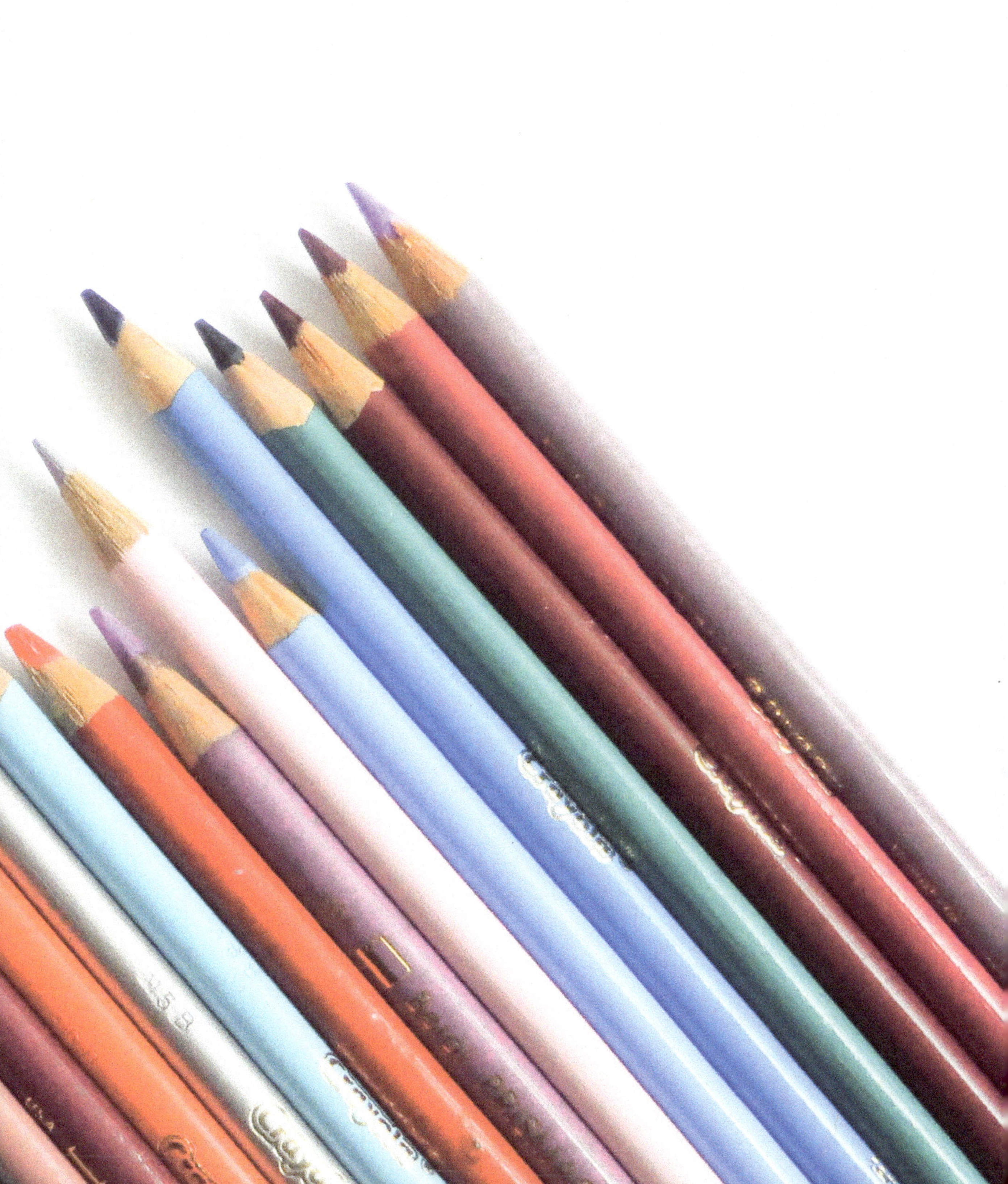

# what is a creative retreat?

First, let's redefine "retreat."

A retreat is any amount of time you set aside to pursue your creative passion(s).

"Any amount?" you ask. Yes. Of course, going on a daily retreat for two hours would be really nice, but realistically, you may only have ten minutes to write, grab your pen, and go. The purpose of a retreat is to exercise your creative muscles, to keep you limber mentally, and to move you forward in your creative practice. Coupled with the realization that this moment is a gift, you truly can transform even the smallest, most mundane opportunities into a creative retreat.

That's what this workbook is all about. It's your guide to preparing for a retreat, including ideas of what to do or experiment with, exercises to stretch

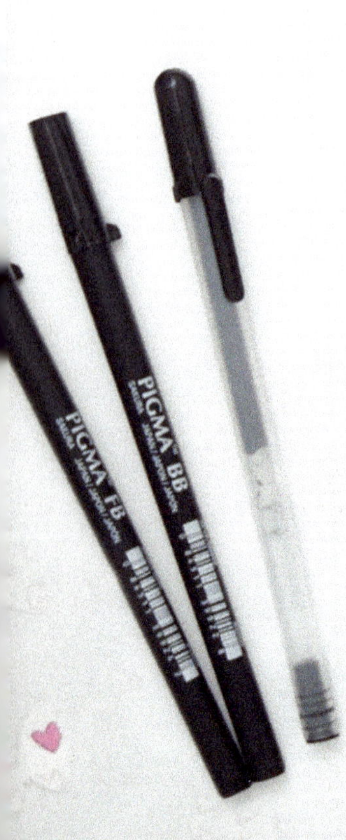

your creativity, and what to do when you come home or have to get back to "real life." Mountaintop experiences are wonderful, and if you ever get a chance to go on a weekend creative retreat, then I'd say, "Go for it!" But in order to build a creative life, you need more than those once-a-year (or lifetime!) experiences.

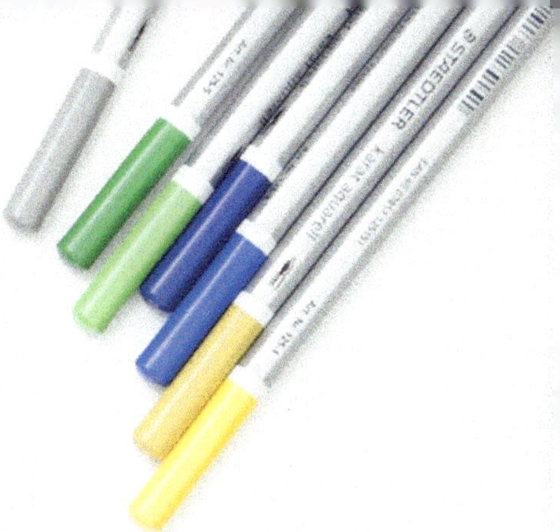

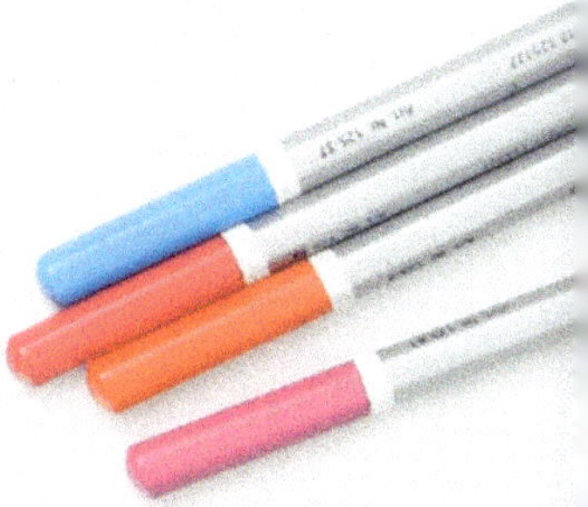

Throughout this workbook, you'll discover space to write your goals for your creative practice, exercises to stretch you, and interviews from various creative women. It's meant to be a companion on your creative journey, a place where you can dream big and jot down ideas. It's a place for you to be refreshed, to remember what makes you laugh, and to encourage you to reach out and share your gifts with others.

Enjoy!

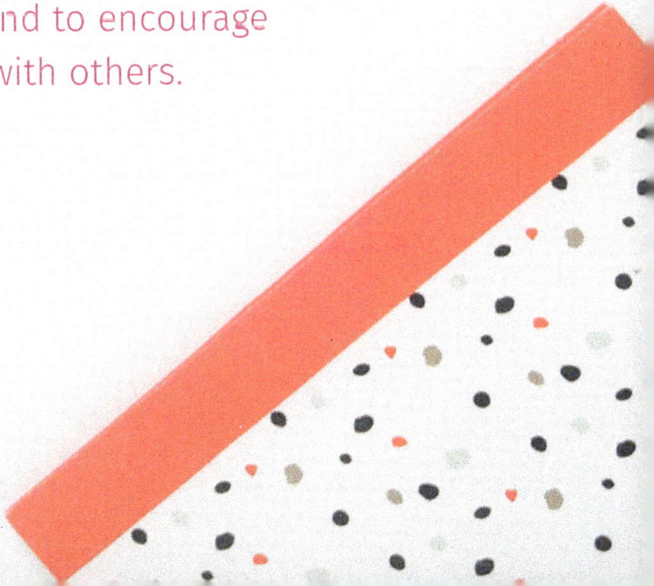

alas for those
that never sing,
but die with all
their music in
them!
- oliver wendell
holmes

# you need a retreat

Unless you received this workbook as a gift, you probably agree that you need a retreat. Even so, it's easy to let life get in the way and convince us a creative retreat is a luxury and not worth our time. When you're tempted to put this workbook on the shelf and forget about your initial excitement about doing this for yourself, remember these three reasons you need a retreat. Hopefully they'll help you put a firm date on the calendar.

**1.** **A retreat will recharge you.** It's your time to invest in your creative goals and projects. But it's also a gift to your friends and family. Why? They love you and all of your quirks and foibles, but honestly, giving them a refreshed, joyful, and energized you is a gift.

**2.** **You will complete projects** because you've made them a priority. I don't know about you, but I really like finishing a project. By setting goals on the worksheets in this book, you'll be able to see measurable results. Who knows, you might finish those Christmas gifts you're always wanting to make early this year!

**3.** **You will grow as a person.** This is your time to try new things and learn. On some of my retreats, I end up reading more than creating, and that's a good thing. Sometimes we get so busy we forget to invest in our personal growth. A retreat makes space for that. Whether your focus is finishing projects, adding some margin to read and learn, or just taking a breather and thinking through some of your goals, a retreat can bring you deeper clarity and help you greatly.

> By setting goals on the worksheets in this book, you'll be able to see measurable results.

# permission

## Let your creativity escape.

Some of us don't like to "mess things up." We like things new and perfect. A blank page, whether it's in the form of a new sketchbook or the empty pages of this workbook, feels intimidating. So before we get started, let me tell you a secret:

**You can't mess this workbook up.**

If you need to, write or draw a little note to yourself below to remind yourself to enjoy this process. This workbook is your guide to dream, plan, and grow your creative practice. Have fun!

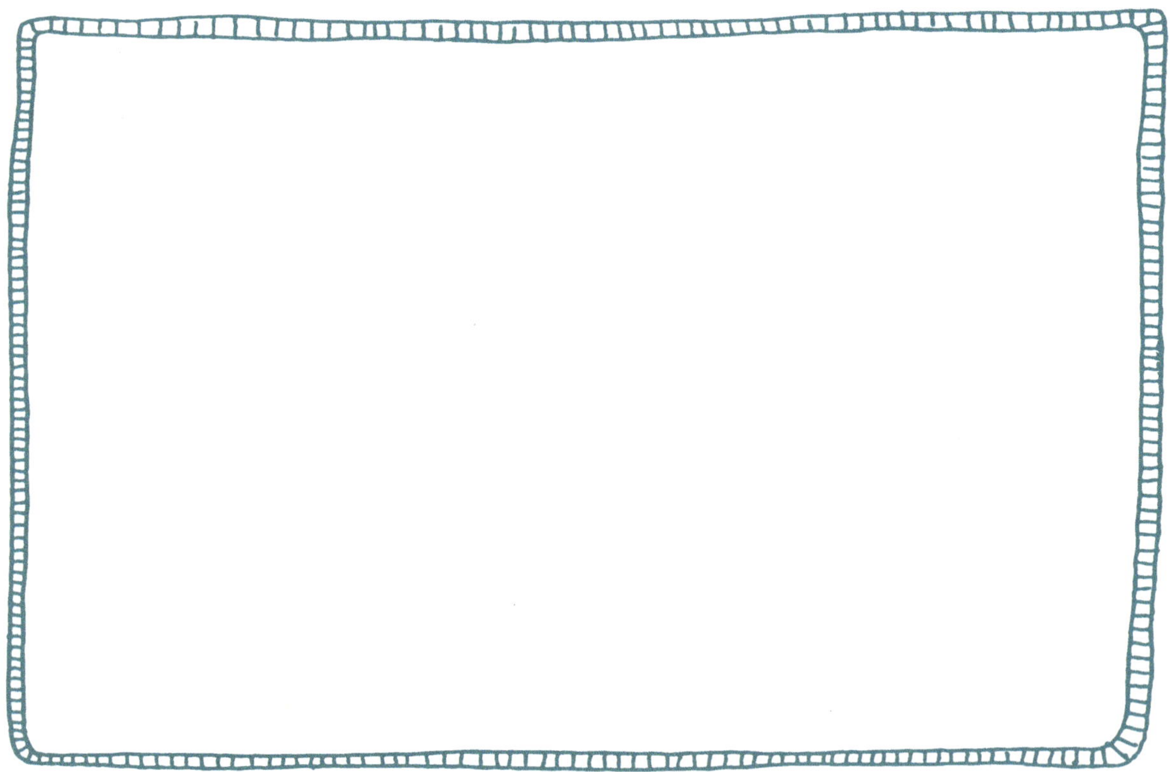

This permission page was inspired by the amazing Lauren of thinkingcloset.com.

And here's a coloring sheet in case you like to color.

# PERMISSION TO CREATE

I am a creative person. It's important to me that I take time to create, to work on my projects, and to have fun. I hereby give myself permission to create!

X ______________________________

Date: ______________________________

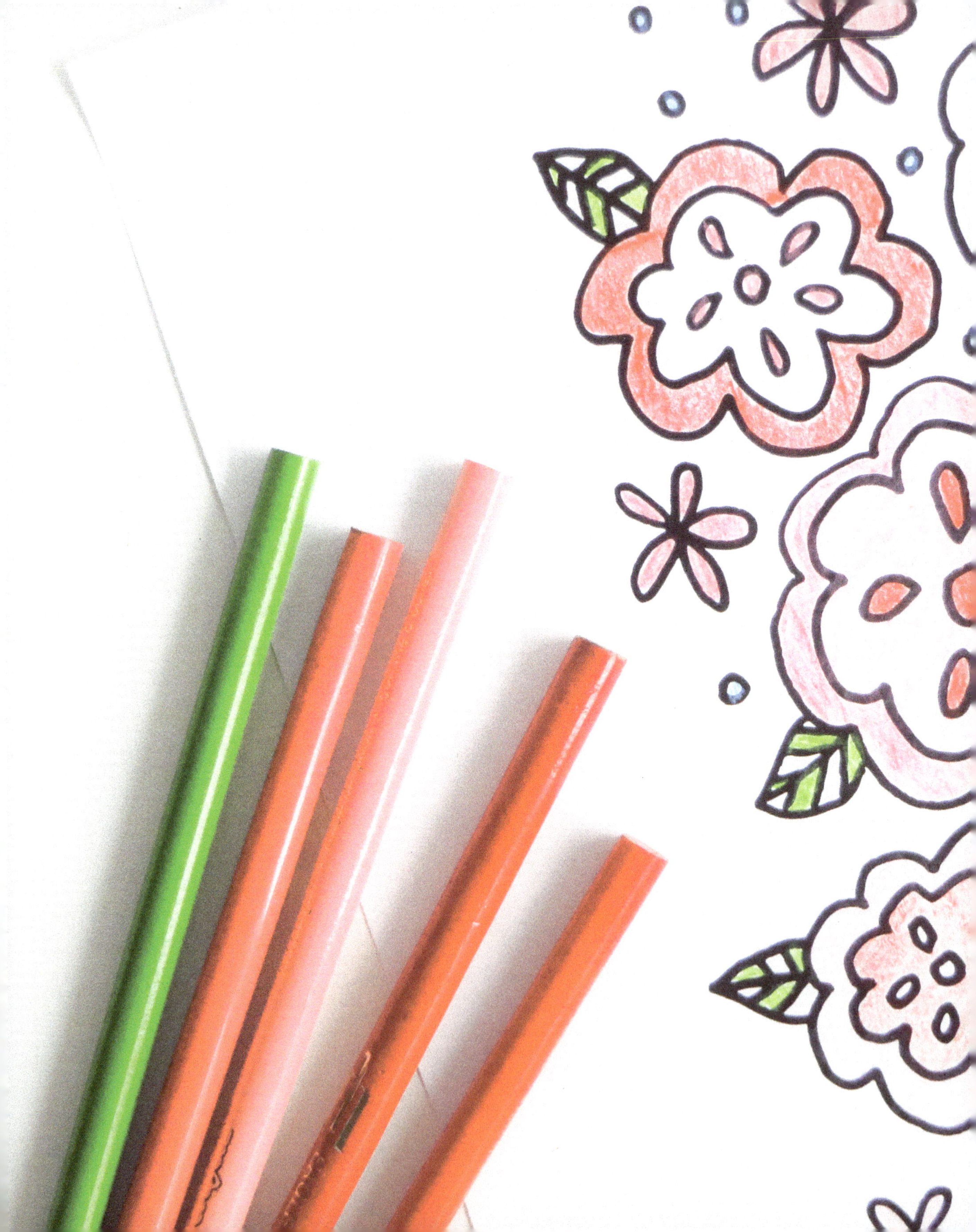

## Colleen Meredith

Wife, Mom, Nana, Sister, Teacher,
Art lover, Creative



**Describe your business or mission.** Each day, I am compelled to recognize and celebrate the beauty I find in my world. The form it takes varies: a journaling moment, sketching a branch, decorating my home, watercoloring.

**What does a creative retreat look like for you?** My creative retreats are seldom planned because I tend to be impulsive when a creative urge strikes! When an idea comes to me, I will stop and jot it down or make an attempt at it right then and there. If I can get my idea/observation recorded, I can go back and work on it later. When I interrupt my life with a few creative moments, the satisfaction of doing what my heart is asking gives me joy.

**How do retreats benefit you?** My mini-breaks from life to indulge in a sketch or a journaling moment, for example, give me a sense of happiness and connect me in a deeper way to my world. That small act of expressing my interpretation has created a thread of connection with every place I have lived. It provides a release of an idea, which I find satisfying, surprising, and enjoyable.

**Any advice for someone who is just starting out with taking personal retreats?** Start today. Don't wait for the "right" time because it will seldom arrive. Respond to the impulse to create. If that means jotting the idea for a sketch, writing down that string of thoughts brought on by the tiny birds in a bush, do it. For me, when I look at these written ideas, inspiration to complete one (or more!) begins to take hold. Give yourself permission to bring your creative idea to life. Making a date to spend a longer amount of time on a creative project can be deeply satisfying. Don't cheat yourself of time, give some to your creative self.

# "IF ONLY I HAD MORE TIME TO CREATE"

I used to dream about How Nice It Would Be if I could be independently wealthy so I wouldn't have to work and I could make things all day long. It sounded like a dream come true... I knew I would own a studio by the ocean with a white picket fence and buckets overflowing with nasturtiums. It bugged me that I had to get up every day and be a secretary. All of that LOST creative time! I felt that at the very least, I needed a job in a creative field — you know, so I could be a REAL creative.

But slowly I began to learn a few things:

ONE - There is no shame in making an honest living even if it isn't your "dream job."

TWO - Yes, 40 hours a week is "The Man's," but the rest of the week was mine to make my Dream LIFE.

**THrEE** – All of those years of working informed my creative process. It taught me to observe, to learn when I felt like being lazy, and to follow through.

I learned to **DRINK IN** the moments I did have to create. And how to jump straight into the creative flow.

Basically, I learned that for **MOST of US**, this is exactly how creativity happens. Most of us are...
- painting on the weekend
- writing at lunchtime
- finishing an embroidery during naptime
- making a card after school

# AND YOU KNOW WHAT?

That's perfectly okay. You can **thrive** there. Let's not resent hard work, okay? Let's accept it as training ground AND provision so we can afford to create. And let's continue to dive in and explore our creative projects.

# A QUICK-START GUIDE to CREATIVE RETREATS

1. Write down **FIVE** things you love to make and/or that make you happy.

2. Pick **ONE** thing.

3. Choose a date in the **NEAR** future for your retreat. Incorporate a reward if you need to.

4. Make it an **EASY WIN**. The point of a creative retreat is to pause from the busyness of life and enjoy your creative side. **HAVE FUN!**

# a sample schedule

- **The night before, pack a bag of supplies and write down the goals you have for your retreat in this workbook.** (Turn to pages 22–23 for the goals section.) Doing so will help you tomorrow. You also might want to read through some of the exercises and thoughts in this workbook and tag the pages that you would like to do on your retreat.

- **Leave the house at a specific time so you don't waste the morning.** This might be tough—if you're anything like me, it is very easy to put off things you love and need. If you have children, you can prep things for them to do the day before or write a list to help your spouse or babysitter. Be sure to get enough rest the night before your retreat.

- **Head to a place where you can have some time alone.** This might be a coffee shop, the library, or a neighborhood park.

- **On your way, listen to music that inspires you and/or pray that God will speak to you and bless your time.** Think of ten things that make you smile or ten things that you are thankful for right now.

- **In no particular order, work on a project, read your Bible or an inspirational book, journal, or sketch.** Enjoy your treat and beverage as you do so.

- **Go on a walk.** Be aware of the beauty of the ordinary. Think about what you learned, whether in your reading or creating. Take pictures. Pray.

- **Go back to your car and drive home!**

A couple of thoughts here. Since we're all different, you might want to walk first to get your energy out or freewrite (dump all of your thoughts with no edits) into a journal. You may find that taking deep breaths and closing your eyes for a few minutes prior to starting your retreat will help you focus.

Decide ahead of time what you will work on since it is easy to waste time when you're on a retreat. You can also schedule in time to waste if that helps you. (In other words, tell yourself you can people-watch, write your to-do list, or procrastinate for fifteen minutes—then you'll start.)

> Be aware of the beauty of the ordinary. Think about what you learned, whether in your reading or creating.

# supply list

## What to bring on a retreat

These are some of the items I bring in my bag for a creative retreat. You can add or subtract from these to your liking.

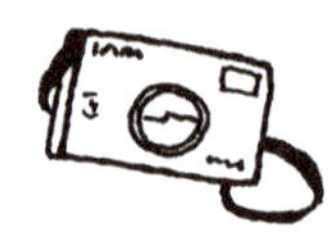

- ☐ **One or two projects and their supplies.** For a short retreat, bringing more means you'll likely be distracted rather than getting something done. It's a good idea to bring a new project as well as something you've been working on for a while.

- ☐ **Camera.** I bring my camera for taking pictures of the beauty around me and for gathering inspiration.

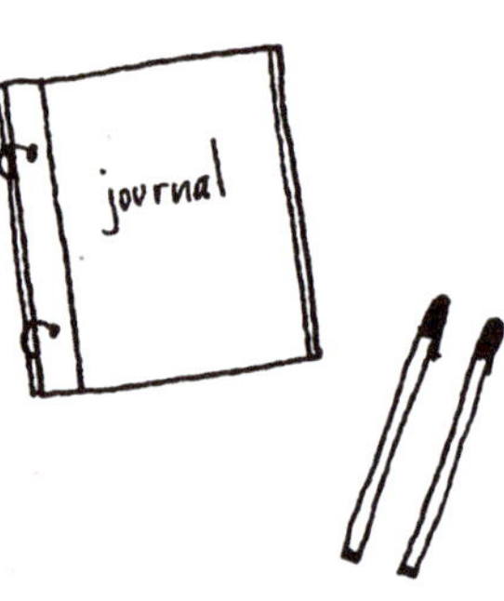


- ☐ **Journal.** I use a journal to write my thoughts down during the retreat as well as list ideas of things to work on later.

- ☐ **Pens/pencils/watercolors.** I have a small box of portable watercolors that are perfect for retreats.

- ☐ **Bible or inspirational book.** Reading the Scriptures is a huge encouragement for me. Sometimes I'll end up working on a little hand-lettered piece from a verse that stands out.

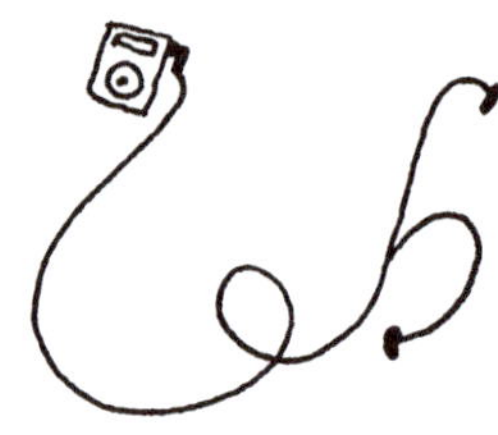

- ☐ **Walking shoes.** Usually after I work on my projects, journal, and read for a bit, I need a walk to process what I've learned.

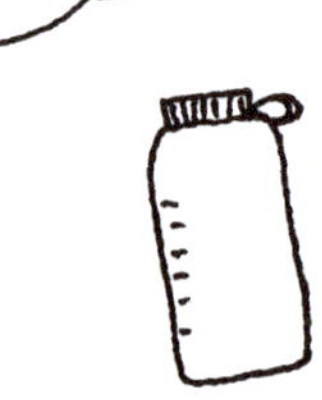

- ☐ **Music.** I don't always bring music on my walk, but I definitely enjoy listening to music in the car on the way to and from my retreat.

- ☐ **A snack, a treat, and water.** These are essential for working on projects (at least for me!) I don't want to go home hungry or have to break up the little retreat time I have to go buy a snack.

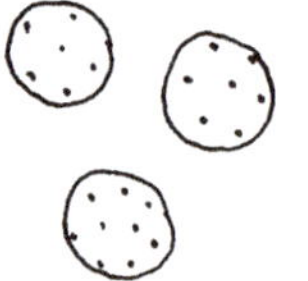
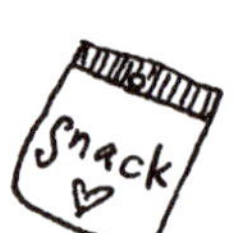


- ☐ .......................................................................................................
- ☐ .......................................................................................................
- ☐ .......................................................................................................
- ☐ . .....................................................................................................

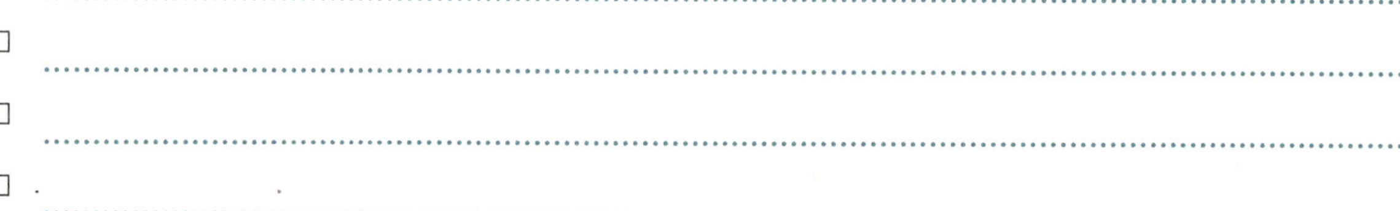

# Lauren Lanker

The Thinking Closet
http://www.thinkingcloset.com

> **"I'm on a mission to help you break down the walls that stand between you and your creativity. Let's do this!"**

**Describe your business or mission.** I'm on a mission to help you break down the walls that stand between you and your creativity. Let's do this!

**What does a creative retreat look like for you?** My husband and I have decided to set aside a 24-hour period each week where we "rest" from work, email, and social media and seek life-giving activities. Sometimes that means seeking out time with friends, with each other, or on our own. For my alone time, I always opt for a creative retreat! It might involve reading a book, making something with my hands, writing a letter, or meditating on scripture through art worship in my journaling Bible. Carving out this time each week hasn't been easy, but it has been so incredibly meaningful for us both, we make it a priority now.

**How do retreats benefit you?** When I do take a break from my work routine in order to refuel my creativity, I find I am the best version of myself. And I'm an even better worker when I return back to the tasks before me because I'm not running on empty anymore. The creative tank is full. My body and soul have found their strength again. Personally, I am a much happier, much easier-to-live-with person, more vibrant and alive!

**Any advice for someone who is just starting out with taking personal retreats?** Some of my first encounters with creative retreats were enjoyed with a kindred spirit. So, I'd recommend reaching out to a friend or family member and planning an hour or two of creative retreat time to spend together. You might read side by side or share a palette of paints as you work on your own projects. Or perhaps you want to read aloud together or work on a shared project. It's up to you! I just find that having a trusted friend participate in a creative retreat WITH you can make it all the more sweet. (And less intimidating.) Also, I love Jennie's reminders in *The Creative Retreat* that you don't have to leave home to experience a creative retreat and it doesn't have to be long! Even a twenty-minute burst can refuel the creative tank when spent intentionally. You've got this!

## Use this space to brainstorm your first creative retreat.

- Why do I need a personal retreat right now? (Your "why" can be very motivating!)

- What will I do on my retreat? What will be my retreat's purpose? (Working on a project, reflecting, etc.)

- When will I go on my retreat? Where will I go?

LIVE YOUR LIFE LIKE IT'S A MIRACLE... BECAUSE IT IS.

# goals for my retreat

Place sticky notes in the spaces below for your goals. That way, you can easily remove them and add them to your planner or post them around the house as reminders when you return home.

**Two things I will work on in my creative life.**

(example: "I will make time on my calendar each week to create, and I will honor that appointment.")

**One thing I will give up or stop doing that hinders my creativity.**

(examples: "I choose to stop self-sabotaging when it comes to creating." "It's okay to take twenty minutes to work on a project.")

**If you have any other creative goals, add them to these boxes.** Make sure your goals are measurable. Instead of writing, "I want to be more creative this year" write *how* you will be more creative. "I will knit four scarves this year." "I will write 500 words a week." Whatever it is, it needs to be measurable so you will be able to see your progress.

**Remember goals are our friends.** If your goal is torturing you, you might need to either let it go or rework it so it's a help to you. The point is for you to grow creatively. Yes, there are times when growing stretches us and doesn't feel very good, but at your core, you should still love what you're doing.

**Set your intention.** Doing the work of setting goals for your retreat is important because it creates an intention for your time. This is an easy way to track progress in your creative life—you'll set the goals now, and then you'll be able to see growth as you work towards them. You can also set goals that deal with your heart, such as having the intention to give yourself grace and to enjoy your creative time.

# WHO ELSE CAN BE WONDERFUL, BEAUTIFUL YOU?

# your retreat style

## Every person retreats differently.

Use the following pages to jot down discoveries you make about yourself as you find your retreat style. This is one of the reasons why taking more than one retreat is important. You might find it difficult to get into a productive groove if the space you choose is distracting for you personally. Trying new things will help you create the retreat that fits you perfectly.

- What worked for you on this retreat? What would you like to do again?

- What did not work? Why? How could you turn this into a positive experience?

- For your next retreat, what would you like to change or streamline? (Different time of day, fewer projects, easier goal, better location, etc.)

..................................................................................................

..................................................................................................

..................................................................................................

..................................................................................................

..................................................................................................

## Beth Anne Schwamberger

Brilliant Business Moms
http://brilliantbusinessmoms.com

> "Quiet time to have a mini-retreat is like a breath of fresh air. It breathes new life into my business and reduces my stress."

**Describe your business or mission.** We're all about helping moms grow businesses on the side while also spending time with their families.

**What does a creative retreat look like for you?** Right now, it looks like a Saturday morning to myself while the boys go do something together. I'm lucky to have a son in school, so I get a lot of quiet work time during the week.

**How do retreats benefit you?** Having a chance to simply sit down and list out what matters most —my top priorities for life and business—is so key. It helps me get away from just being busy and having a long to-do list and lets me ruthlessly cut the things that simply don't matter. Quiet time to have a mini-retreat is like a breath of fresh air. It breathes new life into my business and reduces my stress.

**Any advice for someone who is just starting out with taking personal retreats?** Start by simply writing down everything that matters to you and everything you'd like to do. Don't filter yourself initially—just write. Then discern the patterns there and use those to determine your top priorities. Get your mind out of "I should" mode and into "I would love to…" mode. Dream big! And eliminate silly things that don't matter.

# stepping out

For some it's an easy choice to decide what to do on a retreat, while others need a little guidance. There's nothing wrong with that. I find myself vacillating between the two, actually. Sometimes I know ahead of time that I'll be working on a writing project and going on a walk. Other times, I flip open a book to find ideas.

In this section, you'll find activities to experiment with as well as of a list of several different kinds of retreats you can try. I've also included space at the end of this chapter for mind-mapping or listing additional ideas that come to you so you'll have them all in one place.

As you step out on this adventure, keep in mind that this is meant to be a continual and evolving process. There's no such thing as a typical creative retreat. On my retreats, I tend to take time to reflect on what's going on in my life at the moment. I've included a few essays to get you thinking about your own ideas regarding creativity, such as the need to be brave and be ourselves as creatives, our creativity and self-worth, and being precious about art supplies (for the perfectionists among us).

P.S. There are plenty of journaling pages in the back of this book for you to write your own essays if you get the urge!

# types of retreats

## Thirteen fun retreat ideas.

**1.** **A letter-writing retreat.** Pack up your address book, stamps, a fun pen, and some cards and head over to a coffee shop (or someplace with a nice view), and write. You will get to relax with a treat and enjoy some time away, and you'll also have the chance to share with others. I personally need to take more of these. I love sending and receiving letters in the mail, but I forget to make the time to write them. Scheduling a retreat where letter-writing is my main focus definitely helps.

**2.** **The stay-at-home retreat.** Sometimes getting out of the house for a retreat is completely impossible. Don't worry, though, you can still have a great time from the comfort of your own home. It is easier to be distracted at home, so be aware of that and plan for it. I recommend cleaning your house or retreat space beforehand so you'll have a clutter-free retreat experience. Work while everyone is in bed or away. Make sure your supplies are all ready, and make your snack and get your tea or coffee ready ahead of time. You're also going to want to write out some sort of schedule or retreat to-do list to stay on task. I recommend turning off your computer and phone (if possible) since it is easy to want to "quickly check" your email and let your retreat time evaporate. All of that said, the nice part about a stay-at-home retreat is you can wear your comfy yoga pants and get an extra cookie from the kitchen if you run out.

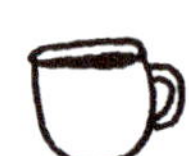

**3.** **The project-focused retreat.** This is the kind of retreat I go on the most. I pack up a project or two and head off somewhere to work for a few hours. I've learned that having a rough schedule for myself helps me accomplish what I've set out to do. Otherwise, it can be easy to waste time and realize I really didn't do much at all when it's time to go home.

**4.** **The devotional retreat.** Pack an inspirational book or Bible, some encouraging music, and your journal for this retreat. Sometimes we need this time to sit down to think through what we're going through and to receive encouragement from Scripture and other devotional writings. This kind of retreat is a great way to feed your soul.

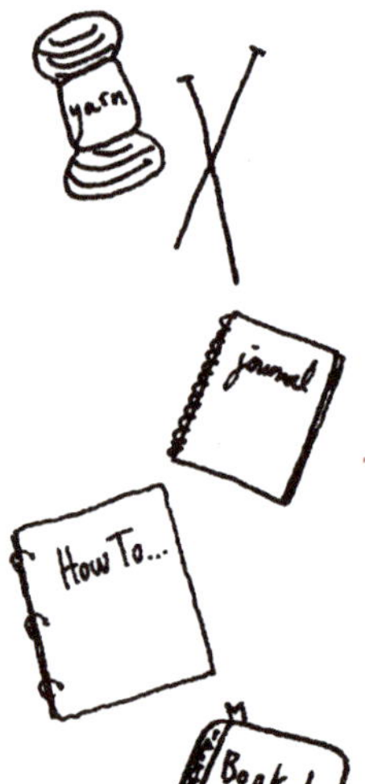

**5.** **The learning retreat.** Maybe you're like me and you have a list a mile long of things you want to learn…someday. On a learning retreat, bring a book you've been wanting to read or a workbook that has been gathering dust on your shelf.

You could also bring your computer and take a class if you'd like. Making time to learn new techniques or ideas is always good for your creative life.

**6.** **The photography retreat.** This retreat is fun and very easy to plan. All you need is your camera and some good walking shoes. Oh, and a snack and water, too. Pack everything in a light backpack and drive to a place where you can walk. Consider visiting a lovely neighborhood in your area, a business park with a quiet lake, a bustling downtown area, or a quiet forest trail. The point for this retreat is to look for beautiful things that make *you* smile and to document those things by taking pictures. Taking the time to slow down and really enjoy and see your surroundings can be incredibly enriching.

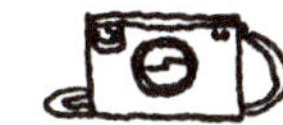

**7.** **The business retreat.** Work on your business plan and goals or brainstorm ideas for the future. Sometimes getting away for a few hours and really thinking through your business can help you redefine your purpose and clarify your strategy. These are great to do on a quarterly basis as a check-in time for your business.

**8.** **The map-making retreat.** This is a unique way to record memories and to think creatively. Take a piece of paper and draw a map. It can be a real map of your favorite places or it can be imaginary, like a map of creative goals you want to accomplish. (Use the map on page 59 to draw your creative journey!)

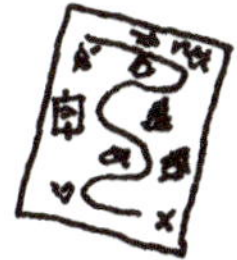

**9.** **The tourist-in-your-own-town retreat.** Often we don't really experience and enjoy our own backyard unless someone is visiting. When I moved to Los Angeles, I told myself that I would be a tourist as much as possible and enjoy that city. To date, I lived there longer than any other place I've ever lived. And I LOVED it. I think, among other things, it was because I made an effort to be on the lookout for fun places to explore. If you need to, use Google or a local travel blog to find an interesting neighborhood to explore in your area. Take your sketchbook and camera—you never know what is going to inspire you.

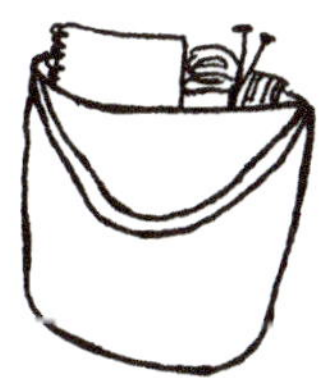

**10.** **The inspirational retreat.** What inspires you? What makes you come alive? For this retreat, take a morning or afternoon and do that thing that fills you up to the brim. Everyone is going to answer this question differently, but here are a few ideas: walk down the boardwalk at the beach, go to a nice coffee shop, walk up and down the aisles at a farmer's market, or spend some time in a used bookstore—preferably one that has a nice, comfy chair to curl up in!

**11.** **The discovery retreat.** This one is slightly different than a regular photography retreat in that you will be taking pictures that follow a theme or have a double meaning for you. Pick a theme before you go on your retreat and photograph pictures that follow it. Consider taking a picture of your shoes to symbolize the journey you're on, a photo of a stop sign to remind you to stop doing something, or a picture of a tree to remind you to stand tall and be courageous. Later on, you could use these pictures as prompts for writing or art journaling. You could also use one of the one-word prompts on pages 54–55 for writing, art journaling, and picture taking.

**12.** **The cooking retreat.** Maybe you love the feeling of kneading bread and carefully rolling out pastries, but you don't have time to do it. Like the rest of the retreats, you'll need to set aside the time and assemble your ingredients. Choose some music and pour yourself a glass of wine or a cup of coffee and make that delicious creation! The best part is that your snack is what you make!

**13.** **The writing retreat.** If you're a writer or an aspiring writer, it really helps to set aside focused time to write. Otherwise, you'll find that life moves merrily along, and your dream will stay that—a dream. Depending on your personality, you might want to go someplace quiet where you can think and write. I personally love reserving a room at our local library; it's quiet and the views are beautiful.

**Write any extra ideas you have in the space below:**

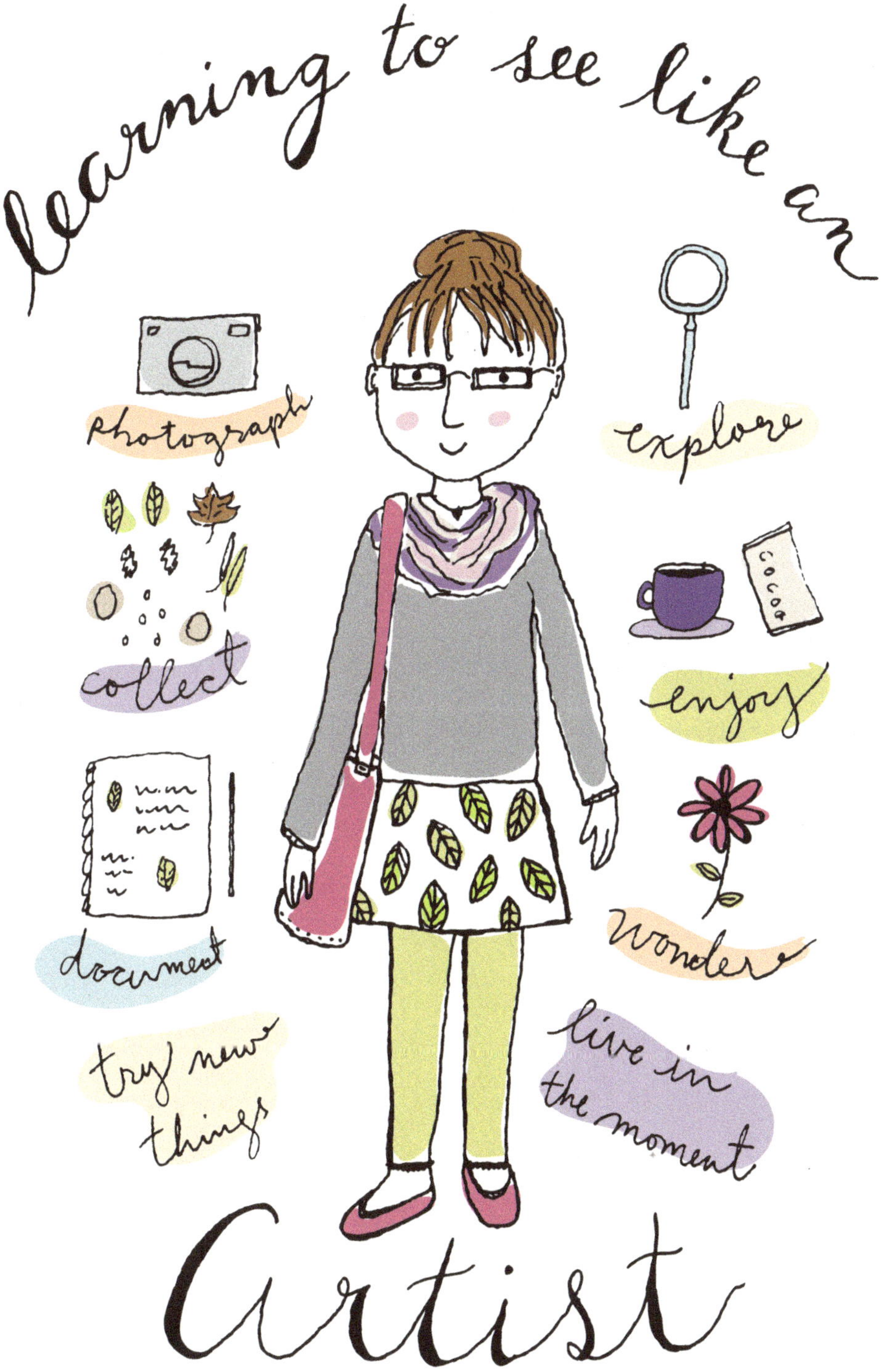

learning to see like an
photograph
explore
collect
cocoa
enjoy
document
wonder
try new things
live in the moment
Artist

# activities to try

## Here are some ideas to try.

- ☐ **Draw your day.** You don't have to be an artist; you could draw stick figures of what you're doing and what's happening around you.

- ☐ **Paint with watercolors.** You can find many watercolor tutorials online. A small set of portable watercolors can go with you anywhere.

- ☐ **Hand-letter.** Draw a quote you really love.

- ☐ **Journal.** Write down the thoughts and dreams you have for your future. Don't censor or edit yourself. Just write.

- ☐ **Origami.** Some people find it very relaxing to fold paper into cute little shapes. You might be one of them!

- ☐ **Cross-stitch or embroider a sampler.** I enjoy simple embroidery projects that I can whip up in an afternoon. One of my sisters likes to stitch gorgeously detailed cross-stitch pieces that take her months to complete.

- ☐ **Make a mini-book.** A mini-book is similar to origami in that you're folding paper, but you get to decorate it with quotes, collages, drawings, or whatever you like!

- ☐ **Knit or crochet.** These projects are great to work on while on a retreat.

- ☐ **Create a collage or art journal.** You can easily create simple collages or work on your art journal while on a retreat. I recommend putting the paper elements, glue stick, and other supplies in a Ziploc bag so they are easy to access (and to put away.)

- ☐ **Write.** A retreat is the perfect place to finally start or finish the book you've been wanting to write. If you're just starting, outline your book's topic and use your retreat to write a couple of sections at a time.

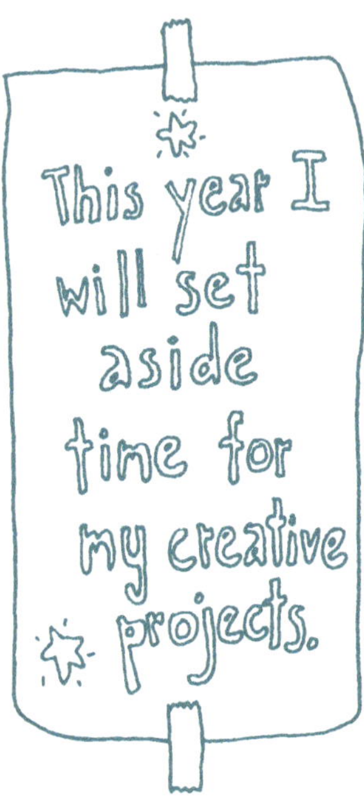


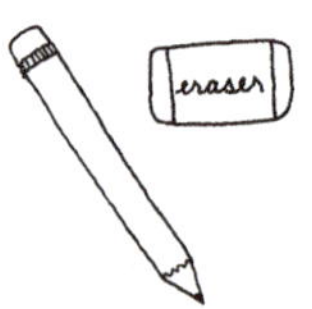
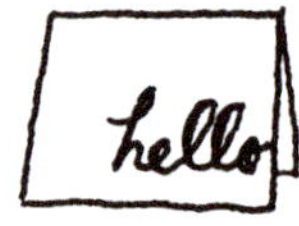

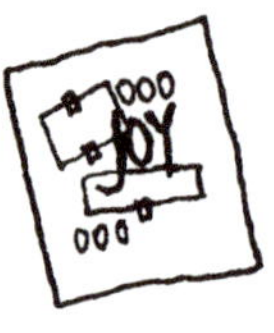

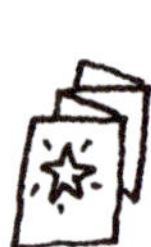
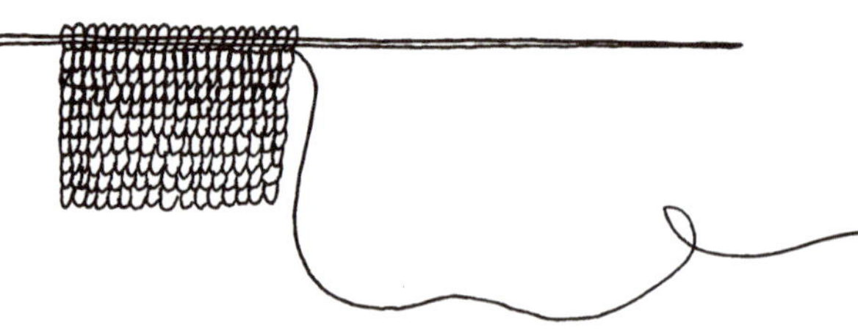

# Include some activities you've always wanted to try.

- ☐ **Gardening.** For many people, gardening is a very relaxing endeavor.

- ☐ **Sewing.** Finish those sewing projects you've been meaning to get to, or start a new one.

- ☐ **Painting with acrylics.** Get the paints out and have fun!

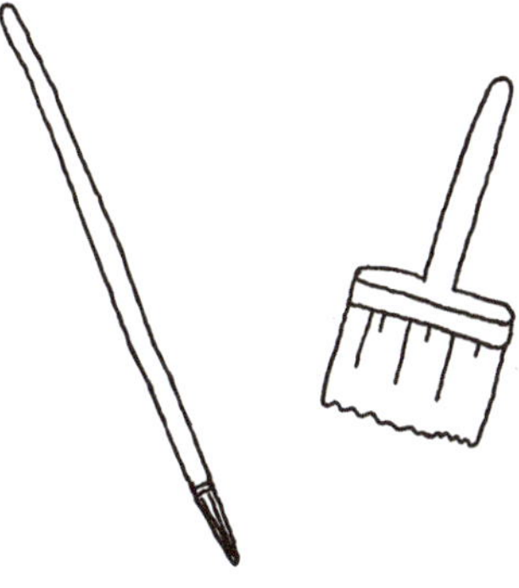

☐ ......................................................................

☐ ......................................................................

☐ ......................................................................

☐ ......................................................................

☐ ......................................................................

☐ ......................................................................

☐ ......................................................................

☐ ......................................................................

☐ ......................................................................

☐ ......................................................................

☐ ......................................................................

☐ ......................................................................

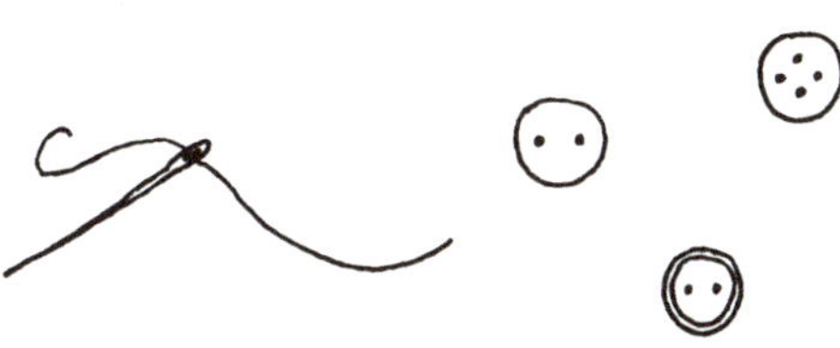

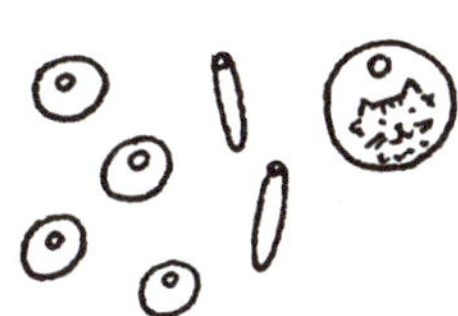

# mind map your ideas

Do this exercise when you're completely stuck and can't think of which project you'd like to make. I'm guessing you've completed a few crafts and art projects in your life. **Make a mind map below to name every single one that you can remember off the top of your head.** As I did this exercise (pictured on the right), I remembered projects I made long ago and always meant to do again. Soon I had an idea for my project. Have fun!

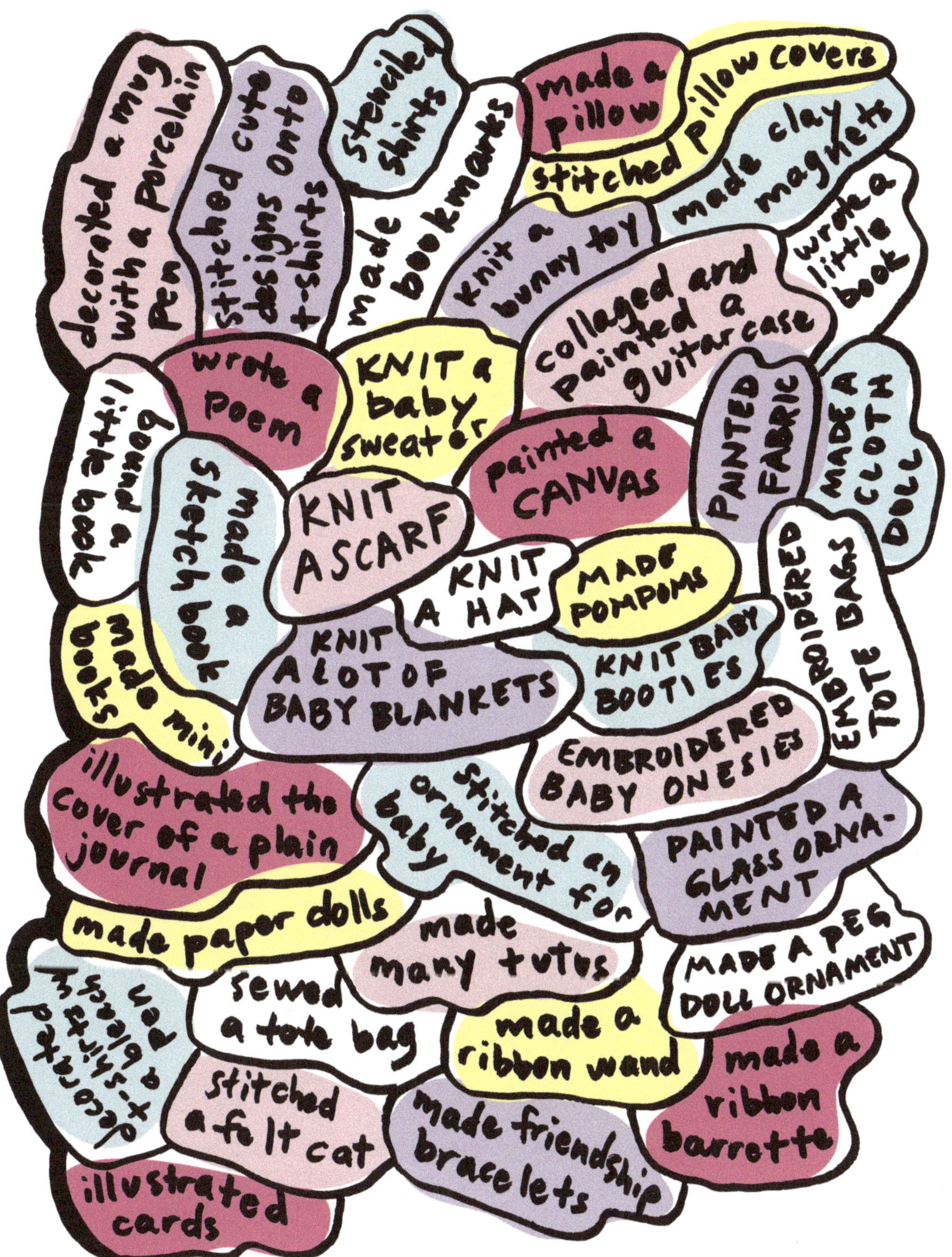

decorated a mug with a Porcelain Pen
stitched cute designs onto t-shirts
stenciled shirts
made bookmarks
made a pillow
stitched pillow covers
made clay magnets
knit a bunny toy
collaged and painted a guitar case
wrote a little book
wrote a poem
KNIT a baby sweater
bound a little book
made a sketchbook
KNIT A SCARF
painted a CANVAS
PAINTED FABRIC
MADE A CLOTH DOLL
made mini books
KNIT A HAT
MADE POMPOMS
EMBROIDERED TOTE BAGS
KNIT A LOT OF BABY BLANKETS
KNIT BABY BOOTIES
EMBROIDERED BABY ONESIES
illustrated the cover of a plain journal
stitched an ornament for baby
PAINTED A GLASS ORNA-MENT
made paper dolls
made many tutus
MADE A PEG DOLL ORNAMENT
decorated a plain t-shirt
sewed a tote bag
made a ribbon wand
made a ribbon barrette
stitched a felt cat
made friendship bracelets
illustrated cards

## Ellen Russell

Create in the Chaos
http://www.createinthechaos.com



**Describe your business or mission.** I make it easy for parents and teachers to get creative with kids by providing simple, unique papercrafts and activities.

**What does a creative retreat look like for you?** My creative retreats look different depending on how busy life is. When things are crazy, sometimes a retreat is waking up at 4:00 a.m. to spend time getting creative on the computer with Inkscape, or doodling and doing crafts alongside my three boys during the day. When things are more flexible, they look like going to a local coffee shop for a couple hours to write once a month, or spending some alone time listening to music and watercoloring.

**How do retreats benefit you?** For business, creative retreats are what allow me to keep my creativity fresh and not burn myself out. In my personal life, retreats help me to stay sane. Life can get so overwhelming and busy that I forget to make time for myself. When I do make time to slow down, get away, and get creative, it helps me keep refreshed and encouraged when I dive back into the chaos of life. And when mini-retreats happen during the cracks of the day, they also allow me to connect with my boys and help show them what it means to be creative.

**Any advice for someone who is just starting out with taking personal retreats?** Don't put it off or think you're too busy to start making time for retreats. It doesn't have to be perfect; it doesn't even have to be a whole weekend to yourself—just do it as best as you can, and remember that it is ultimately going to benefit and refresh your life.

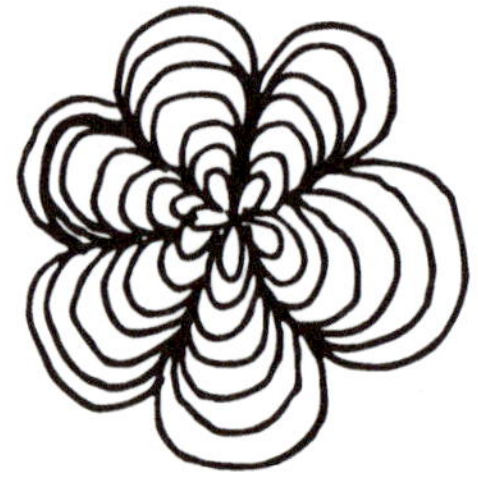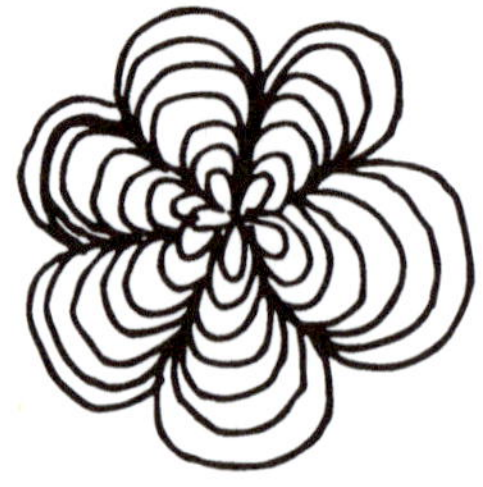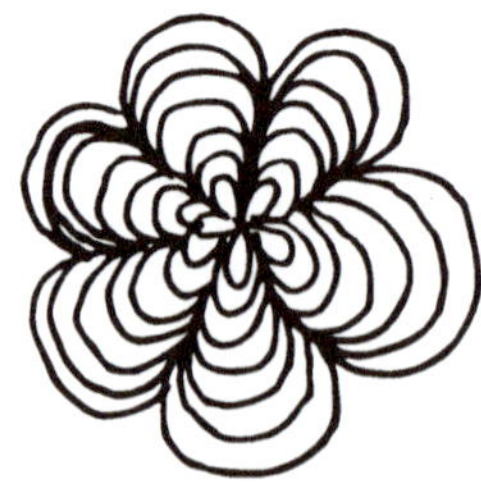

# being brave

Every part of the creative process offers a chance to exercise bravery. Starting the work, pushing through the slumps, discovering new things, finishing a project, and finally, sharing it with others are each in themselves brave acts.

*Understanding this can mean we're kinder to ourselves when the work feels difficult. And when we're kind to our inner artist, we find it easier to extend that grace to others.*

Being brave can be tiring when we set out on this creative journey and then forget to acknowledge our personal feats of courage. Isn't it interesting how we cheer when a child accomplishes something and then ignore our own efforts? Author Tara Swiger regularly talks about the need to celebrate successes and growth as a business owner, but I think this celebrating can (and should) extend to all areas of our creative lives.

Finished a quilt? Got up the nerve to email a magazine editor? Bought your first set of watercolors? Celebrate! Our successes can be big or small, but they need to be regularly acknowledged and encouraged. If you don't treat yourself to a coffee because you just finished knitting your first scarf, who will?

*"You have to be brave with your life so that others can be brave with theirs."*
—Katherine Center

This is one of the reasons I believe your own creativity matters. Your acting on your creativity has a real impact on those around you. It also has a real impact in your own beautiful soul.

One last word of precaution: your courage and my courage will look different. What scares me creatively might not even make you blink. And vice versa. You'll also find as you grow in confidence that certain brave acts will become completely normal while new ones will manifest. Let's do the work of our own bravery while allowing others to do theirs.

*"An ounce of action can crush a ton of fear."*
— Tim Fargo

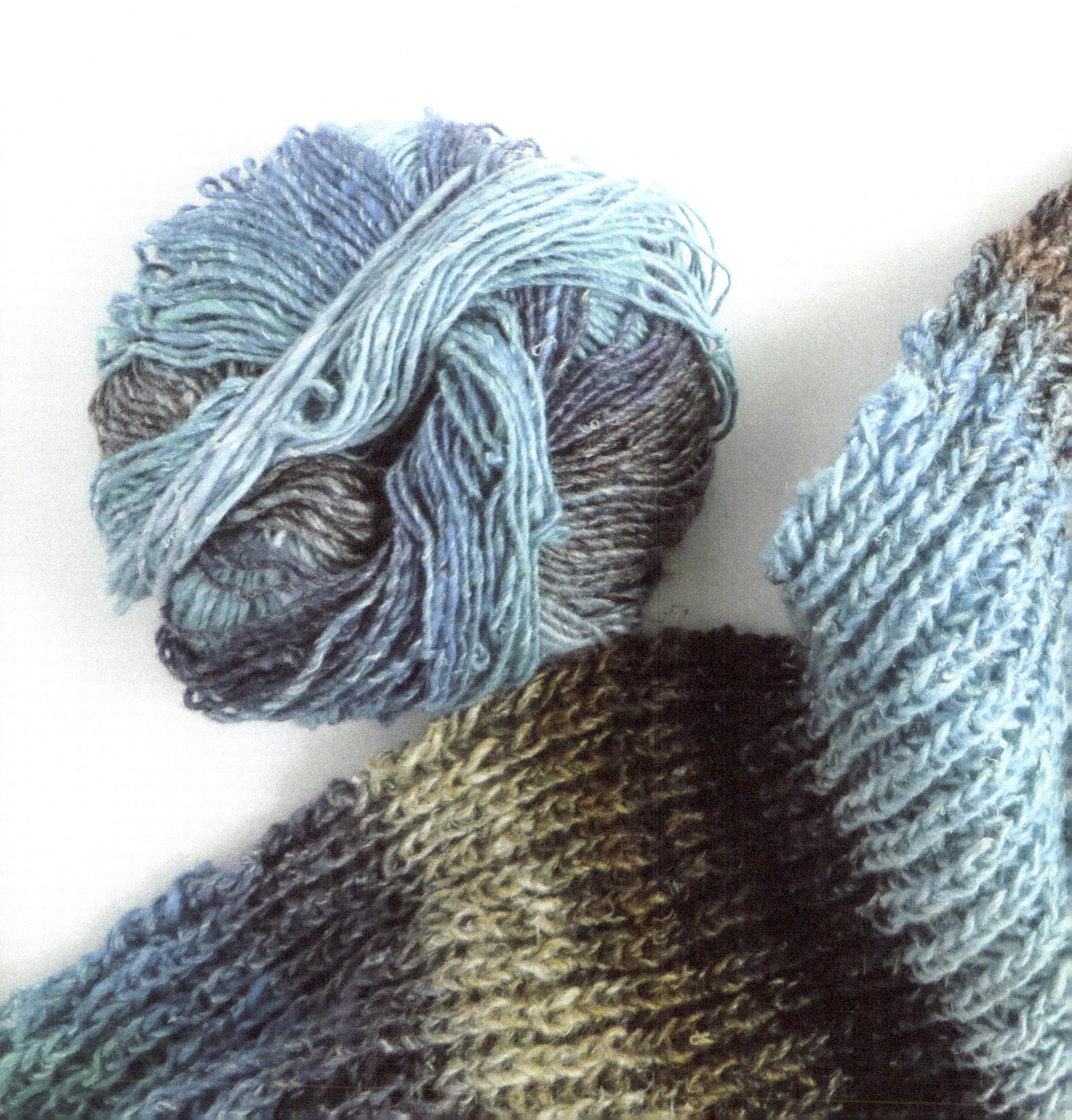

# My Creativity ≠ My Worth

Repeat that a few times. Let it sink in. My creative practice, whether it is a "success" or a "failure," has absolutely NOTHING to do with my worth as a person.

Oooo, this is a hard one, isn't it? We put so much time and energy and love into our projects and when...

the painting looks awful
the hand-lettering is wobbly
the knitted socks are 2 different sizes (!!!)

We feel frustrated. Totally natural. It's okay to feel that way. Where we go wrong is...

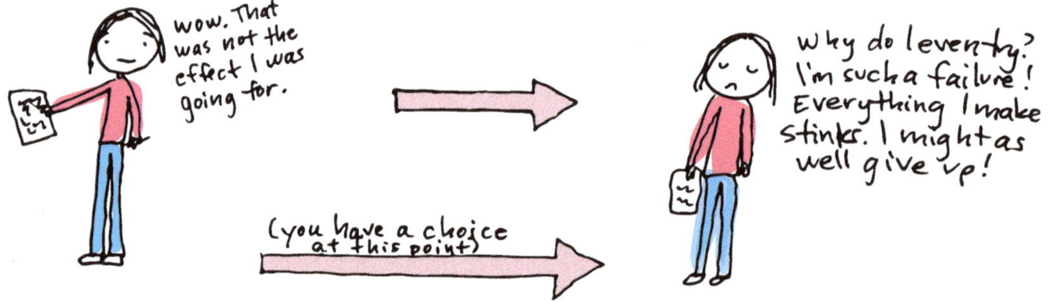


We ALL mess up projects. And the more we try new things, the more we make mistakes. It's all part of the process. It doesn't mean you need

to **STOP** what you're doing. It pretty much
only means you're **HUMAN.** ☺

Whether or not you make pretty, amazing, or
fabulous projects, you will always have worth
because you're a child of God. You are precious
and amazing with or without the rise and fall
of your creative projects.

# ANOTHER WAY TO LOOK AT THIS

is... Would you ever say what you say to yourself
to a little child? Of course not. You would find
the good qualities and encourage them.

# LET'S BE NICE



to ourselves and encourage our creativity to
grow and shine! Who knows how many people
you will impact through your creative
work?

children    parents    neighbors
strangers    friends    students    teachers....

## Tess Arledge

Knitter and designer

**Describe your business or mission.** I guess I might be called a "creative hippy-type" woman, crazy about textiles, patterns, design, and color. My company was called Oliver Handknits, in which I designed and knit individual and unique knitwear for my customers.

**What does a creative retreat look like for you?** Just last week I cleared the decks of other commitments so I could return to having great gobs of uninterrupted time to read, think, and knit.

**How do retreats benefit you?** They are relaxing and stimulating at the same time, and they never create stress, which paperwork and bills definitely do.

**Any advice for someone who is just starting out with taking personal retreats?** Sure, how about this: don't try to make anything the first time, just immerse yourself in colors, textures, books, and others' designs as a stimulus to your own creativity. Enjoy all you see and touch.

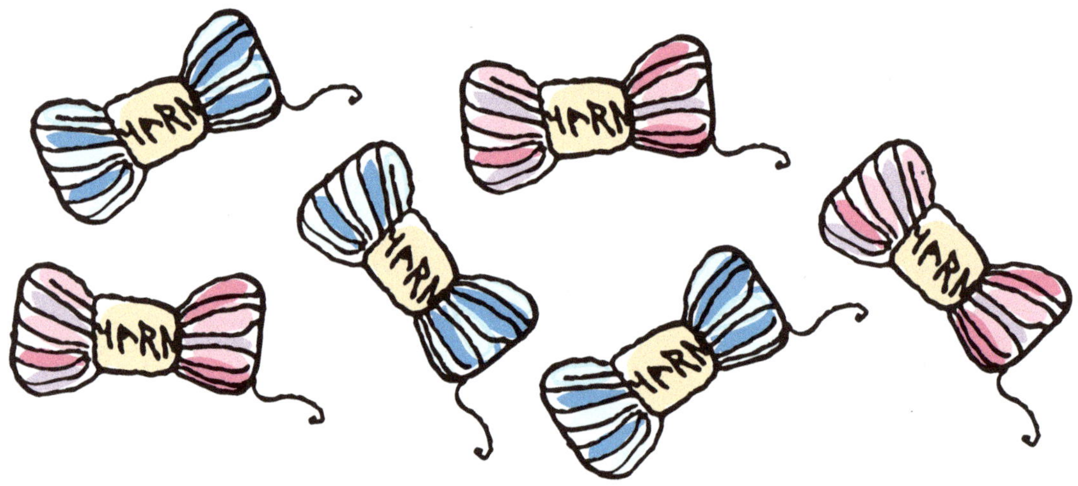

# DON'T BE PRECIOUS.

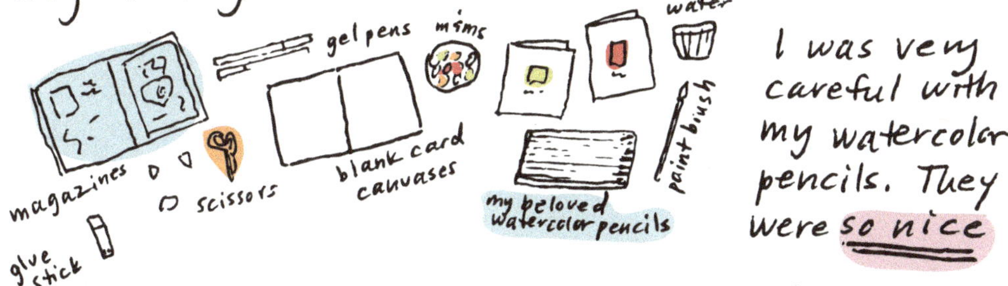

Years ago, I had my first real job, and with the money I made, I bought a small case of watercolor pencils from the local art store. These were the days of Ramen and no furniture, and I was so happy. I would stretch out all of my art supplies on my living room floor and make cards.



I was very careful with my watercolor pencils. They were so nice and I didn't want to use them up. Just like I was never ever able to use the Sanrio stickers I bought in elementary school, they were too nice to be used.

## SO I USED A TINY DOT OF COLOR HERE and THERE

and I was right! Those pencils lasted for YEARS.

I still had that same set when my daughter was born and one day, I opened up the tin case to let her try drawing with one. She held the precious pencil in her chubby fist and scribbled.

**UM, WOW.** That was a lot of color. She was pressing so hard the lead broke. Had that _ever_ happened before? The pencil was just as shocked as I was.

I reached for the sharpener...

And I sharpened the pencil and...gave it back to her. In fact, I took out all of the pencils and showed her how to make grass and sky and clouds and cats. That was the day I took out all of my supplies that had become precious—only for special occasions—and put them in jars. They were our dining room centerpiece for a while.

We began using them. For grocery lists. To-do lists. Coloring. Impromptu art-making.

# I HAVEN'T "ARRIVED" AND I NEVER WILL!

BUT ONE THING I'VE LEARNED is supplies were meant to be used. It's okay to use pencils to their nubs, to spill paint, to scrape the last bits of glue out of the glue stick. It's amazing how much <u>MORE</u> creative our lives have become because we have canvases on the wall beckoning us to quickly paint a bit of texture and because the pens and pencils are all easily accessible.

Being precious with my supplies was the same mind block we get when we can't start a new sketchbook because it's too "nice" or we think we'll mess it up. I say definitely mess it up — use every medium you have on hand OR do what my cousin does — he just skips those first few pages b/c they're a nuissance. <u>Love</u> that.

## WHATEVER THE CASE...

let's all remember that the whole purpose of art supplies is to <u>make</u> stuff. They want to be used up. ☺ So get out those supplies and have fun!

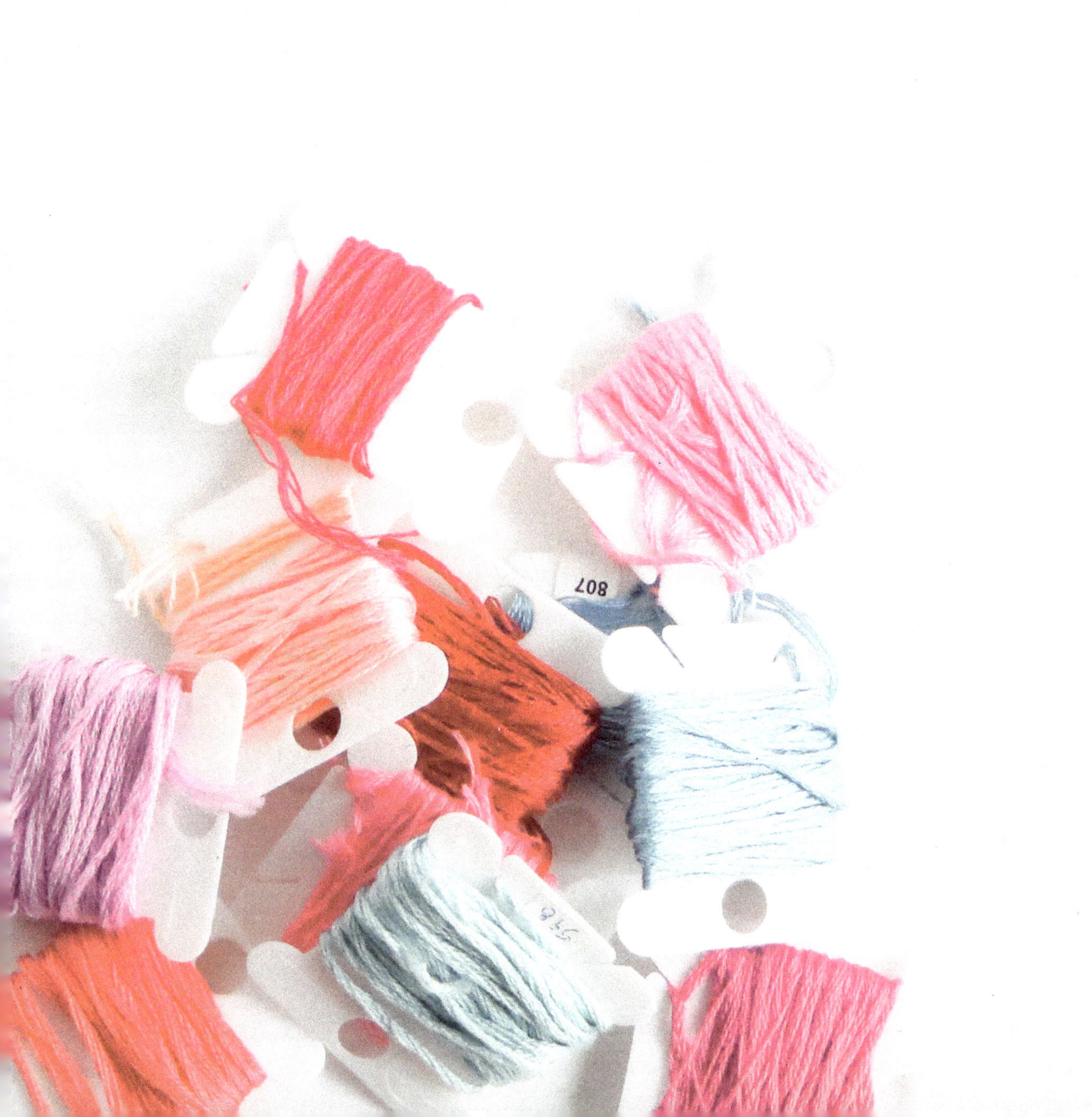

## Ashley Brooks

Brooks Editorial
http://www.brookseditorial.com

> *"Now I schedule time for things that recharge me, like taking walks or reading for a few minutes, and put limits on things that drain me, like constantly checking email or social media."*

**Describe your business or mission.** I'm a mom and wife 24/7, a freelance content marketer and editor during naptimes, one-half of the Chasing Creative podcast evenings and weekends, and a writer and knitter in my "spare time."

**What does a creative retreat look like for you?** Making space for creativity is less about time and more about energy. I used to schedule time for mini-retreats, but I would end up unproductive and feeling guilty because I didn't have enough energy left to be creative. Now I schedule time for things that recharge me, like taking walks or reading for a few minutes, and put limits on things that drain me, like constantly checking email or social media. This way I never let my creative energy run dry, and I can squeeze a few words or ideas into the smallest nooks and crannies of my day.

**How do retreats benefit you?** Producing quality writing online will always help my business since the more pieces I write, the more potential clients are likely to see my name or find my website. But most importantly, taking retreats and making space for creativity makes me feel like myself. I think all moms have that experience of losing themselves in the day-to-day hustle of taking care of the kids and keeping the household running. Creativity is how I find my way back to who I really am, not just as a mom but as a person. It's so fulfilling to have a passion that I pursue simply because I love it.

**Any advice for someone who is just starting out with taking personal retreats?** Don't put too much pressure on yourself to be productive. So much of creativity is just being open to new ideas and experiences. Just because you don't paint a masterpiece or write a novel during your retreat doesn't mean it was a failure. Creativity is worth prioritizing, even if your retreat doesn't yield any tangible results.

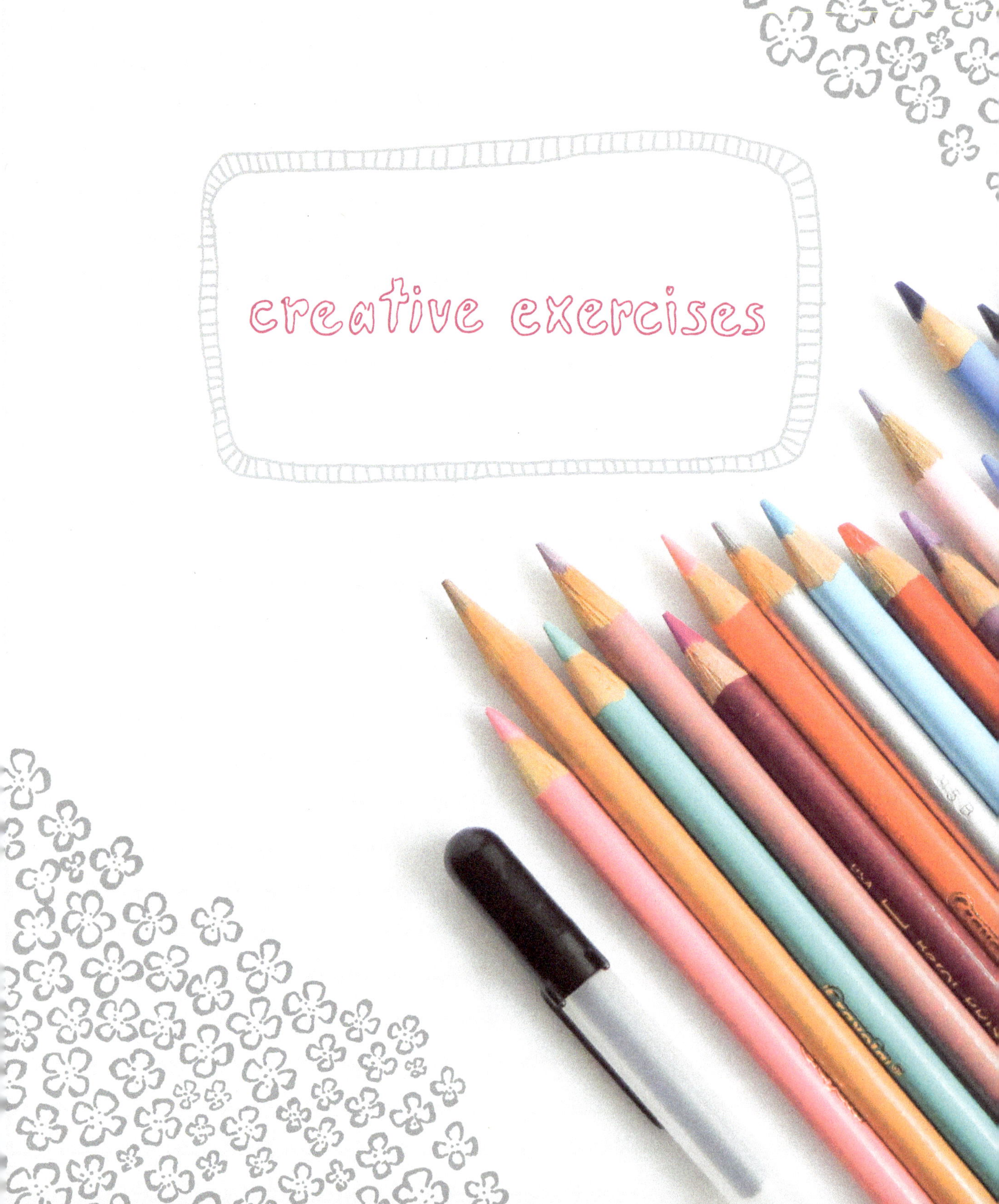

creative exercises

These exercises are meant to be used when you'd like to do some creative stretching. We'll start with several one-word prompts that you can use for all kinds of creative projects. What does the word "abundance" bring to mind, for example? Is there a way you could incorporate those thoughts into a painting or the written word?

Next you'll have a chance to think through the "ordinary things" you see every day. When I think of ordinary things made extraordinary, I think of the artist Wayne Thiebaud, who painted beautiful gumball machines, ice cream cones, and pastries. Never underestimate the power of the ordinary things in your life!

Have you ever mapped out your world? I received a book a few years ago that literally has maps in it that you can fill out. I drew the neighborhood walk I went on every day when my daughter was tiny and a map of memories for my dad's birthday. In this book, you can take a moment to draw a map of your creative journey.

What makes you laugh out loud and what makes you YOU are the last two exercises in this section. Writing what you're thankful for is a great way to reflect on the blessings in your life, and thinking through all the strengths and quirks that make you unique might just help you with that next project. In other words, it's a good idea to bring more of who you truly are into your work.

# creative prompts

Let your imagination soar with these words! Use them as a starting point for projects. You can find things to photograph that match the word you've chosen, you can sketch what one of them means to you— your imagination is your only limit. Have fun!

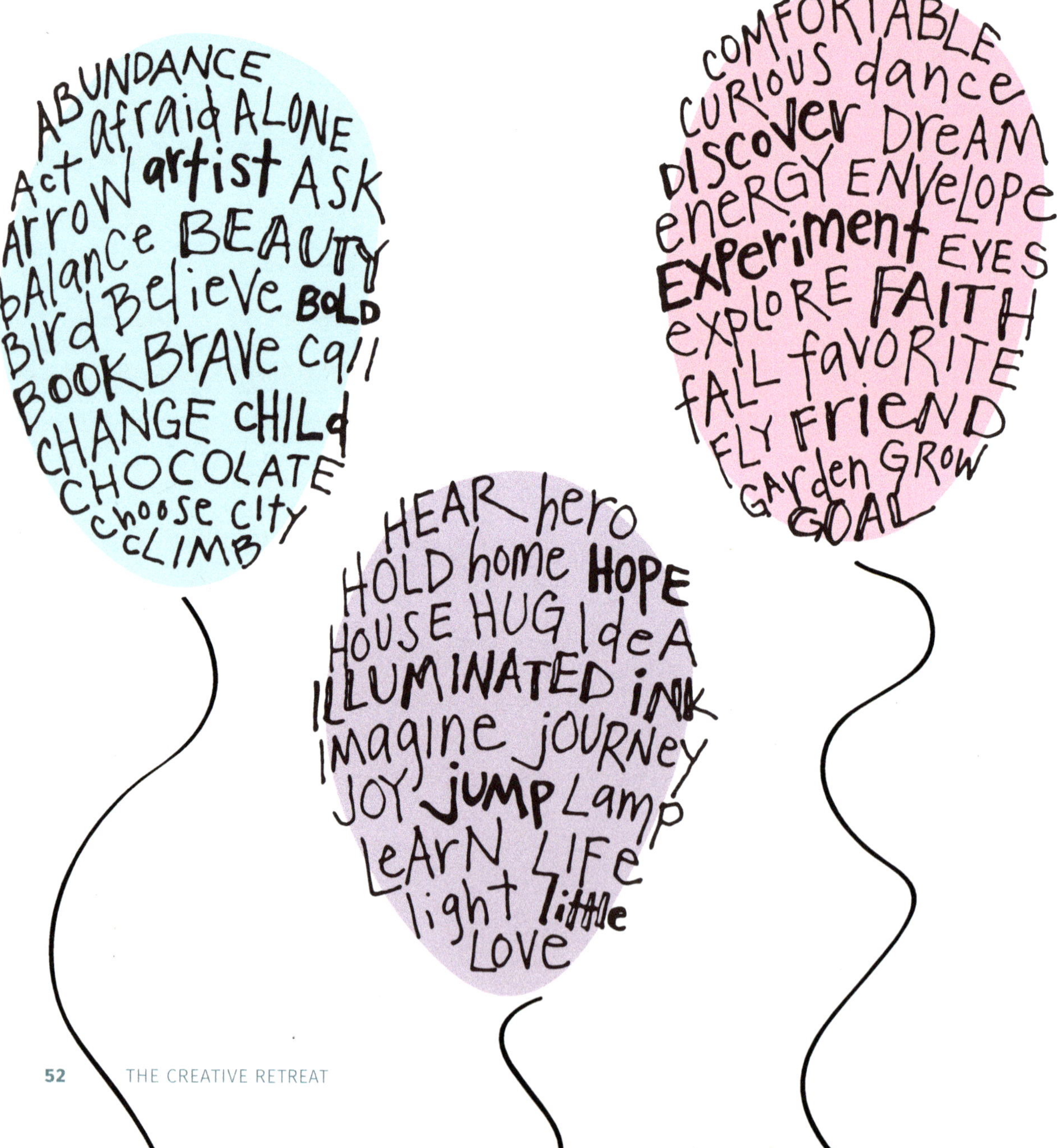

Quote River remember Rock routine SECRET seek SHAdow Run sing smile Sky spontaneous STORY sweet sun time Truth

memory MIND mission Morning New night ocean order PAINT PeAce PERSPECTIVE Place POSSIBLE pretend rain PURPOSE quiet

unIQUE VISIT wait waNder walk whisper TREE wish wonder WILD win VISIT WIND write WOOd you young

# ordinary things

Years ago, I opened a fortune cookie that said,

> you see beauty in ordinary things, do not lose this ability.

I kept that tiny piece of paper and have often thought about the concept of seeing beauty in ordinary things. For this exercise, use these two pages to list or sketch beautiful "ordinary" things.

## Vickie Simmons

I love to create by painting, gardening, sewing, I guess just crafting in general.



**Describe your business or mission.** My mission would be to make what I like and be satisfied that I tried something new and finished it.

**What does a creative retreat look like for you?** There is no making time for creating in my life. If I want to make something or go out and garden, I just have to do it. The housework or grocery shopping will have to wait. I decided not to be a slave to having a spotless house. Not that I don't enjoy keeping house, I just enjoy my crafts and gardening more. It's a choice I had to make so that I could do what I love to do. Thank goodness I have an understanding husband who will pick up where I left off in the house without a grumble. That's been a blessing.

**How do retreats benefit you?** Creativity is my therapy. I lose myself in what I build or plant. I can have quite a nice section of prayer while I'm simply raking leaves. It's a way for me to feel like I'm accomplishing something that others may enjoy or want to make themselves.

**Any advice for someone who is just starting out with taking personal retreats?** Let yourself enjoy whatever it is you chose to do, and don't judge yourself too harshly on whether you did it right. It's that you tried something new and did the best of your ability and learned from it. Sometimes I see something I really want to try and it doesn't turn out like I want. I don't get discouraged but try it again, maybe with a different approach. It's okay if you put it aside. Just don't quit. Pick up something else and try it.

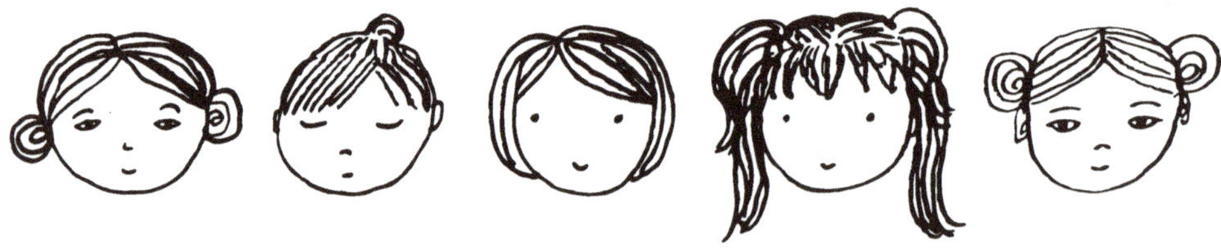

# map your world

Here's a space for you to make a map of your creative journey. Stick figures welcome!

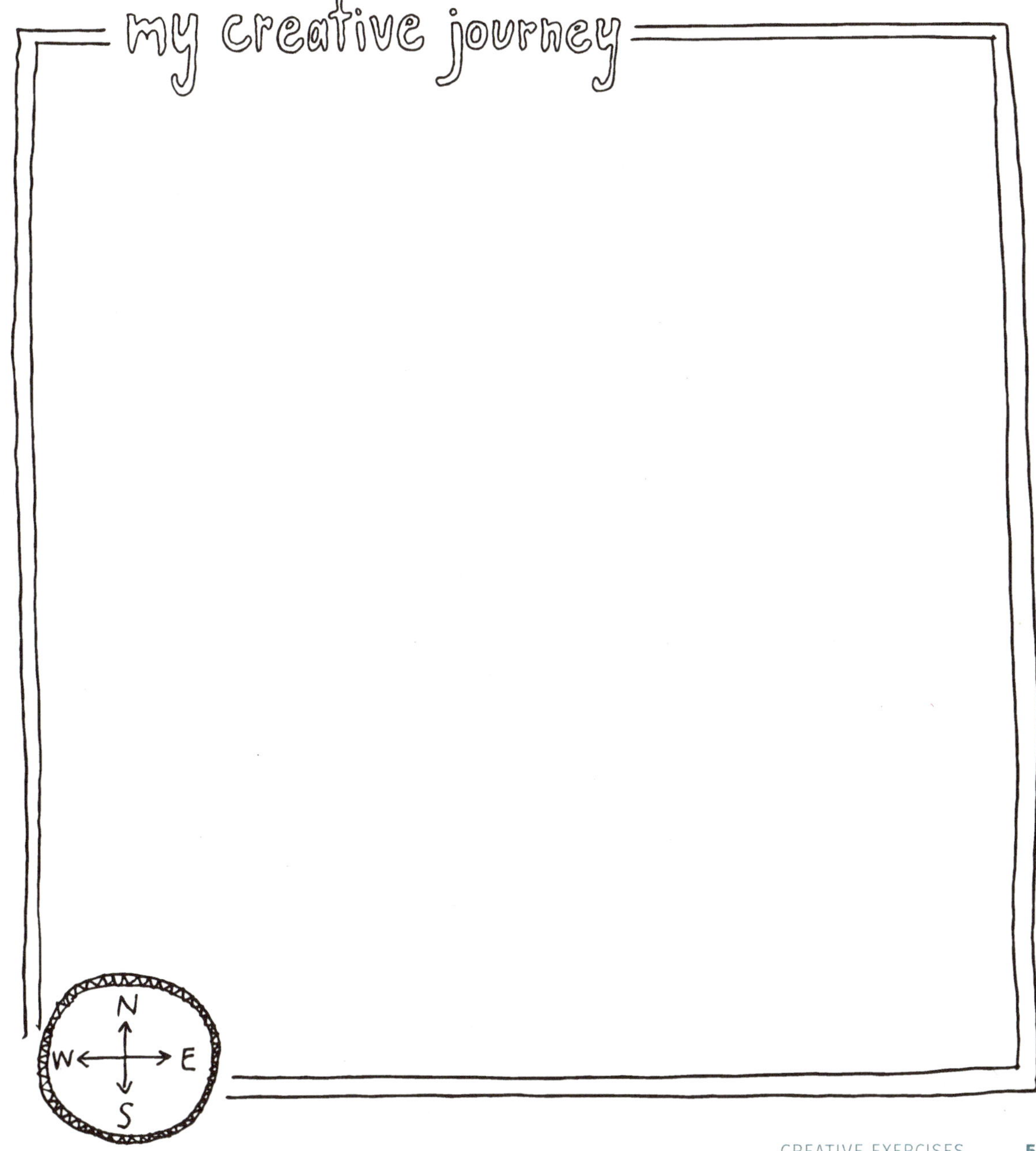

# things that make me happy

What makes you laugh, fills you up with joy, and gets you every time? There are no right or wrong answers here, just fill in the clouds with your thoughts.

P.S. Use these exercises as a jumping point for a sketch, a writing exercise, a collage, or another creative activity.

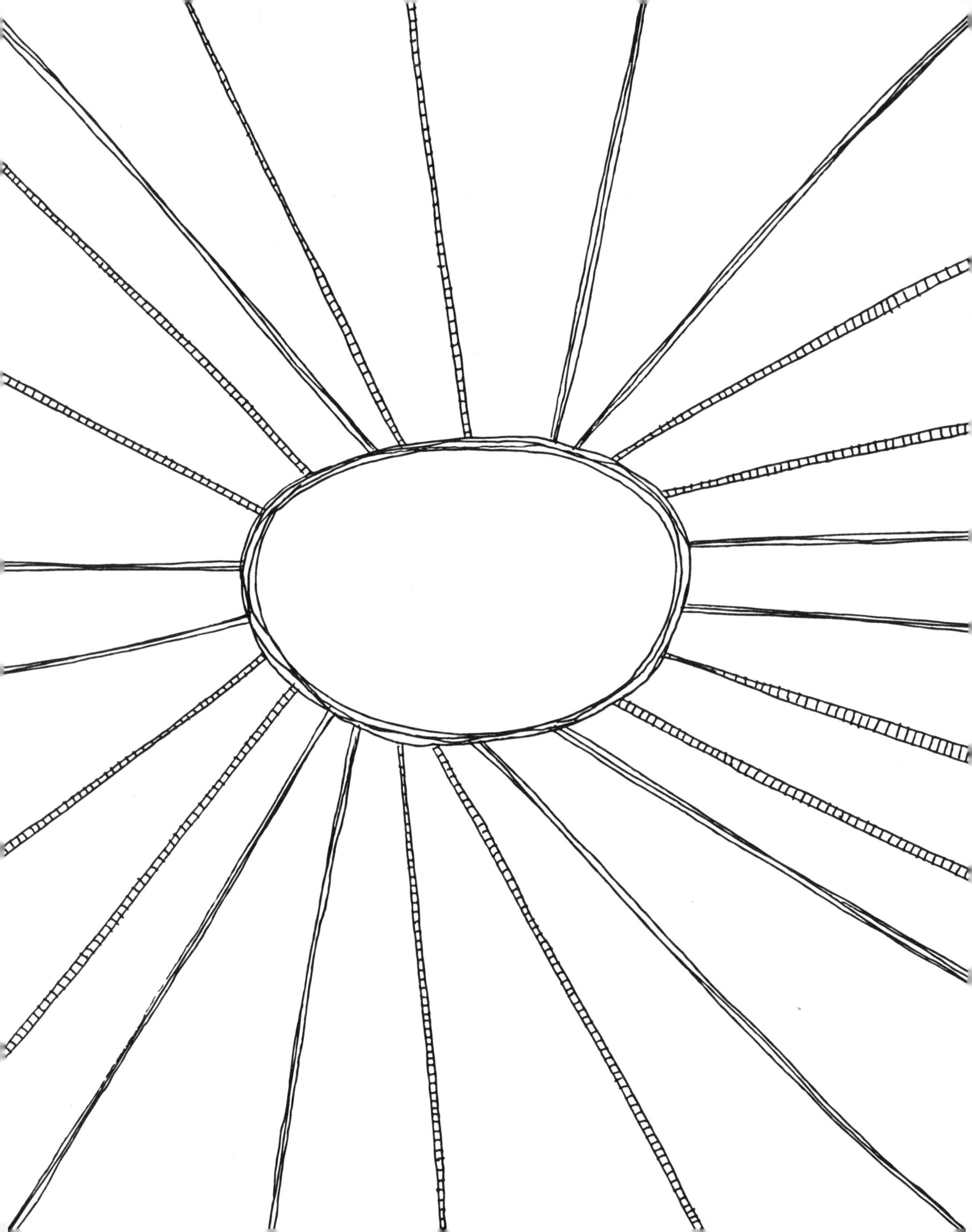

On the opposite page, write your name in the middle circle and fill out the spaces with the things you love, the people in your life — basically everything that makes you YOU.

> **"Anytime I can focus on creative play and experimenting, I feel more excited about everything, really. It's good to step away from your regular routine to get fed new inspiration."**

## Stephanie Owens

Ciccì Coccò Photography
http://www.cicci-cocco.com

**Describe your business or mission.** Filmmaker and photographer. Observer and visual composer.

**What does a creative retreat look like for you?** It helps me to impose some structure on my creative time. For instance, a friend and I have started a "Crappy Story Series" where we have to send each other a short story every week (mostly the kind you'd see for children's books). We call it "Crappy Stories" to remove the pressure of creating something polished and perfect. The point is to get something down on paper, to start exercising those creative writing muscles. Collaborating also helps for accountability. Otherwise, I have a tendency to start projects and not always follow through. I don't see that as always negative; it's good to try to expand your practice by trying new things. But I also think it's helpful to develop some discipline.

**How do retreats benefit you?** Anytime I can focus on creative play and experimenting, I feel more excited about everything, really. It's good to step away from your regular routine to get fed new inspiration.

**Any advice for someone who is just starting out with taking personal retreats?** Accept that your retreat doesn't have to be grand. You don't have to travel to the desert to be inspired. Insisting on lofty perimeters for your retreat can easily turn into a hindrance. It's okay to start small. Sit in a favorite chair or, if you're like me and need to get out of the house, go to a local coffee shop with good pastries. Maybe eventually you'll work up to nights surrounded by cacti and days at the ocean, but even if you stick to your favorite chair—that's great too. Just make the time.

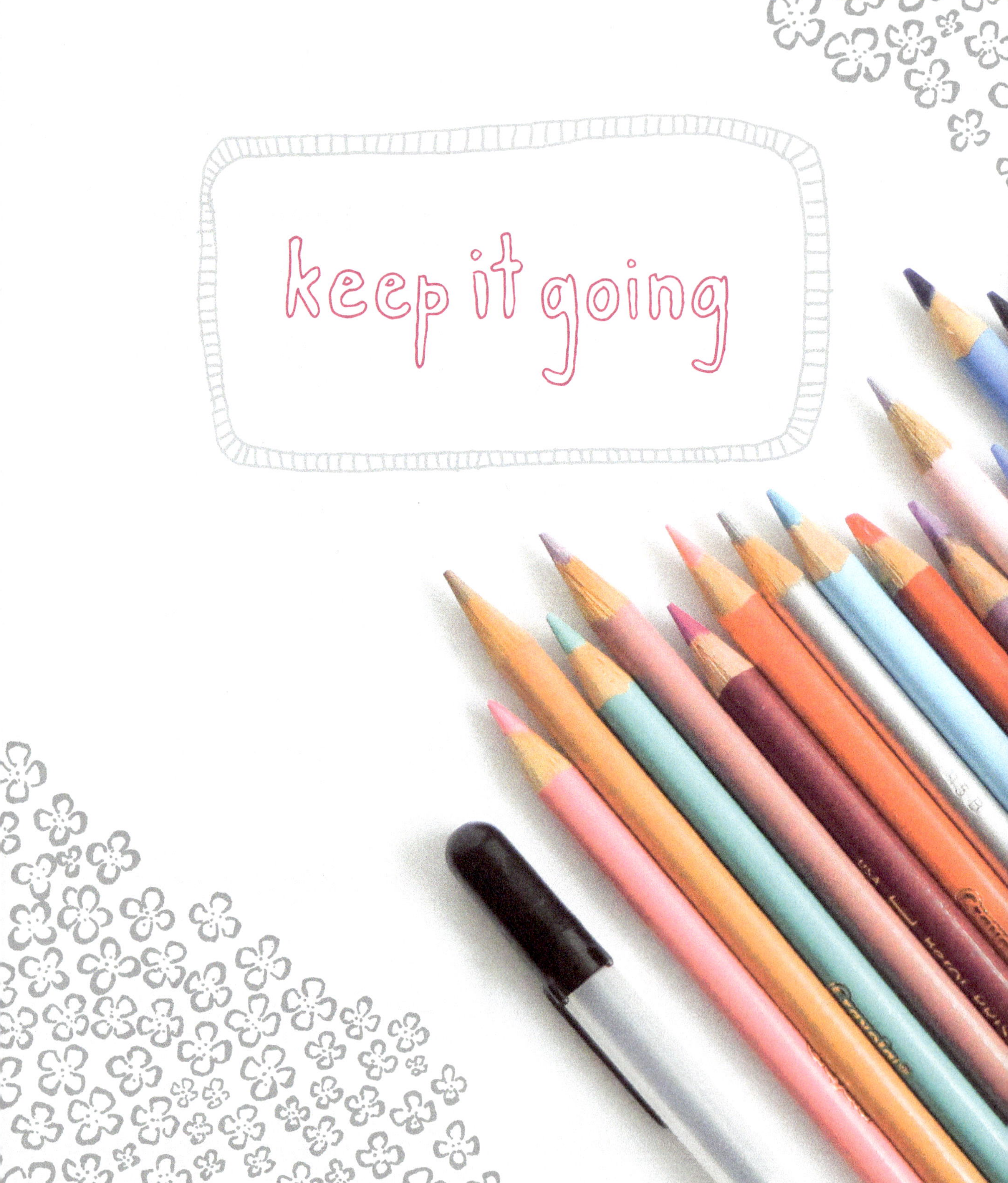
keep it going

The summer before my last semester in college, I lived in a
small mountain town in Colorado and worked at a YMCA. Looking
back, the whole experience seems like a dream. Hiking to
the top of a ridge to see fireworks on the 4th of July (they were far
below us!), holding on for dear life as we crashed through the
rapids of the Colorado River, and sitting on an old tree stump to
journal nearly every morning. That last space overlooked a
field of the most golden wildflowers I've ever seen. It was ah-mazing.

Getting some time alone to work on your projects might have
felt like the rush you get while going through the rapids ("Whoohoo!")
or the peace you might feel as you take in beautiful scenery
("Ahhh"). Whatever you felt as you took your retreat, it might be a
bit difficult to go back to the "real world." In this section, you'll learn
several ways to incorporate what you learned on your retreat
into your everyday life as well as how to sneak in mini-retreats
throughout the day. I call these "micro-retreats" because
they're usually around twenty minutes, but they're sooo nice!

You'll learn how to create an afternoon retreat with your friends
as well as make a plan for sharing your creativity with others.
And you'll also get to hear from a couple more creative women who
have chosen to make creativity a priority.

# continue your retreat

## 11 Ways to extend your retreat

Once you get into the groove of working on a project or being refreshed creatively, it can be frustrating to have to put everything away and go back to "real life." This is one of the reasons why it is important to have regularly scheduled retreats rather than just doing them here and there. You'll be able to see your projects gain traction, you'll see your creative goals being accomplished, and you'll get really good at getting down to business and using the few hours you have in your retreat to CREATE.

That being said, you can also continue your retreat at home by trying these ideas.

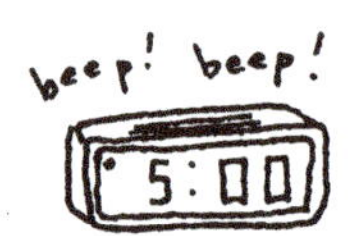


**1.** **Get up earlier.** Just getting up a little earlier than your roommates or family can do wonders for your creativity. As with your retreat, I recommend planning out your mornings the night before so you can make some progress. Otherwise, you might not ever see the benefit. (i.e., Make it a goal to read through a book in a few weeks, draw thirty sketches in a month, etc. This will give you a reason to get up.)

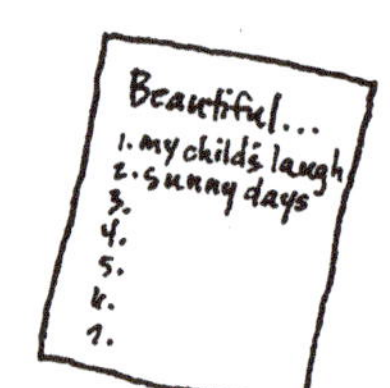


**2.** **Keep a list of beautiful things.** We started this practice in this workbook, but this is a great practice to continue in the days ahead. I recommend keeping a thankful journal—a place where you can write all of the little gifts you receive each day. And there are a lot of gifts—If you have clean drinking water, a bed, clothing, and food, you are blessed. It is not cheating to write, "I'm thankful for a hot shower" each day in your thankful journal.

**3.** **Turn off the computer (and hide your phone).** You can't do this all day, every day, but there are moments when the computer, TV, and phone keep us distracted and busy so we don't create. Checking Facebook for just a second usually takes fifteen minutes. And those minutes could have been used on your creative project. We all get twenty-four hours in a day—use those hours wisely and you'll see extra opportunities to create opening up all around you.

**4.** **Be a kid again.** Kids naturally play and experiment. And now it's your turn. Try something new. Try something that you're convinced you won't be good at. We're creating here. We're playing. We're not trying to solve the world's problems. I love watching children work on their art projects because they are so involved—humming to themselves, choosing colors, busily scribbling away—let's add some of that to our own creative practice, breathing life back into it!

**5.** **Don't compare.** One of the surest ways to stop dead in your creative tracks is to start looking around and measuring yourself up against other people. Somehow we begin to convince ourselves that the world can only hold a certain percentage of creative people, but that is just not true. Fight the comparison monster in your head by choosing to celebrate other people's successes. Allow yourself to have the freedom to make for the sake of making rather than needing every project to be Pinterest-worthy.

**6.** **Get moving.** One of my favorite ways to brainstorm is to put on my tennis shoes and go on a walk. The fresh air, movement, and change of pace have a way of making my brain go into overdrive. I usually bring a scrap of paper and pen to jot down ideas so I don't forget any inspiration. Some people use their phones to write a note or to record a quick voice message.

**7.** **Don't self-sabotage.** This is one of my greatest weaknesses. I love to work on creative projects, but when it comes down to it, I often self-sabotage. I'll write a to-do list that is humanly impossible to complete so I have no time left to work on my projects. I decide to deep-clean the bathrooms and reorganize everyone's closets when all I needed was twenty minutes to finish a stitchery. More often than not, I leave my creative time for the very last minutes of the day when I'm exhausted and ready to fall into bed. Don't follow my example by self-sabotaging. Make the time to work on your creative project and then sit down and do it. Let yourself enjoy this moment.

**8.** **Make a craft bag.** Sometimes what stops us from creating is the effort to take everything out and put everything away again. I put my sketchbook and pencil case in a bag along with the other projects I'm working on. By doing this, I can quickly grab the bag and begin work rather than walking around the house wondering where my daughter put my sketchbook. If you have a larger project or craft, consider how you could store your supplies so they are easily accessible.

**9.** **Set the timer.** Setting the timer for twenty minutes is a great way to work on a creative project when you have limited time. Again, make sure that you have your craft bag or supplies ready, and then set the timer and go. I was so pleasantly surprised at how much I was able to accomplish with these twenty-minute bursts of creativity that I made a thirty-day challenge for my blog readers to do just that. (You can sign up for the free #2030make challenge at www.littlegirldesigns.com/2030make and receive a free mini-workbook and email encouragement.) I'm now a big fan of micro-retreats!

**10.** **Include your kids.** If you have children, think about how you can include them in a creative activity time that will also allow you to work on your projects. Set up a station for them to play at, take out some art supplies for them to experiment with, or do a project together to stretch your own creative muscles. I don't use tempera paint in my own work, but had so much fun one afternoon as I played with my daughter with a set of primary paints.

**11.** **Surround yourself with inspiration.** Quotes, beautiful bookmarks, a brightly colored pillow, and a pretty picture in the kitchen are all ways to keep you inspired. You don't have to spend hundreds of dollars to create a space that is warm, inviting, and that speaks to your soul. Clip themed images to a line with clothespins and hang it up in the living room, or place pictures that make you happy in the cupboards so you see them every time you reach for the cereal. That quote you see every day may find itself in a painting or an art journal collage someday—you never know!

# share your journey

## How can I share what I learned today with others?

A retreat should be a rejuvenating time for you. Even better is bringing something back to share with others. Maybe you'll be able to share a more relaxed version of yourself. Maybe you'll think of ways to incorporate creative time into your daily family life. Maybe you could give your creations away as gifts or teach a technique you've learned to others. **Brainstorm some ideas on this page for how you can share what you learned with the people in your life.**

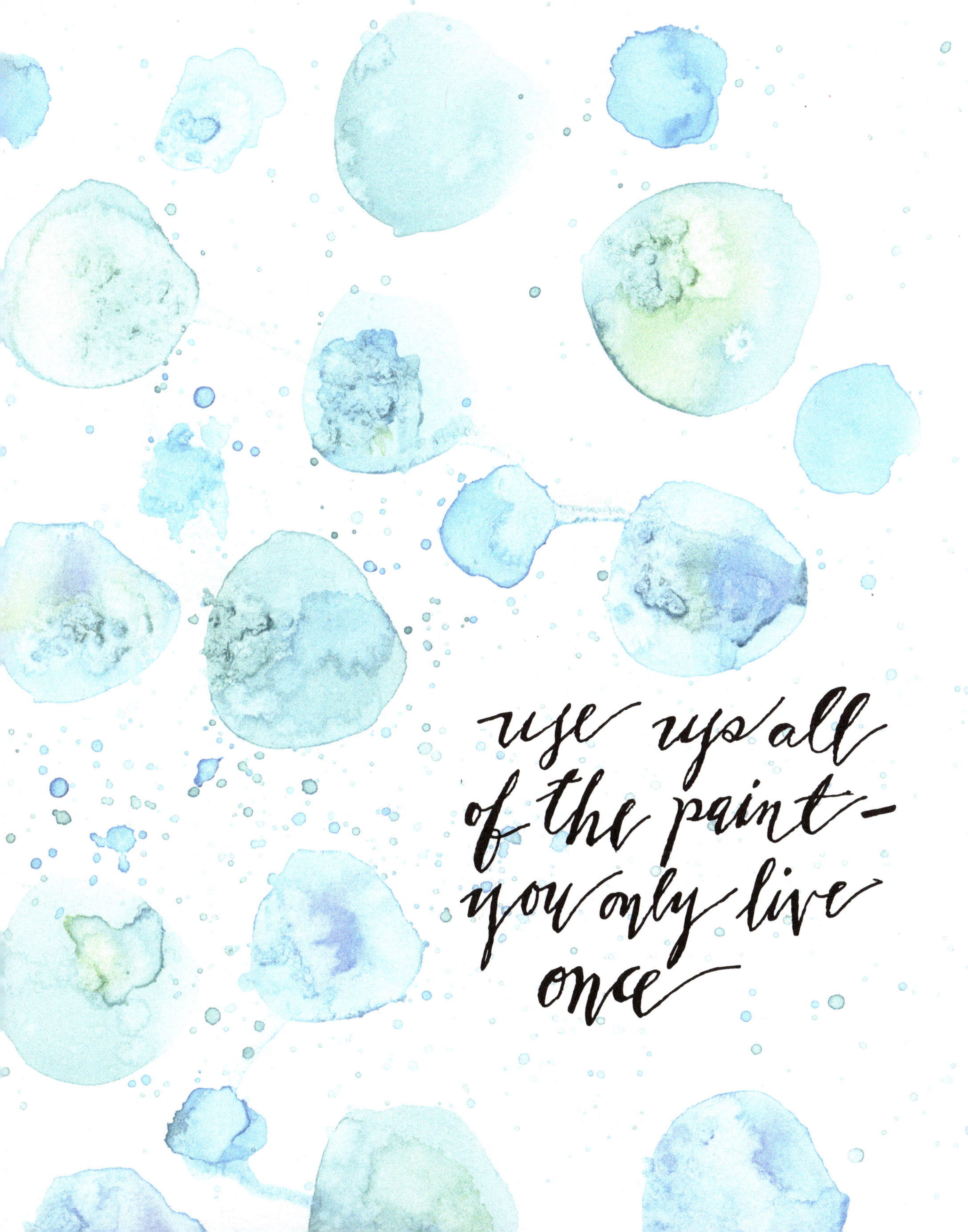
use up all
of the paint—
you only live
once

# friends

## A creative retreat + Friends = FUN!

I love to go off on my own to make things because I can accomplish a lot in a short amount of time, but there is definitely something to be said for sharing your creative retreat with others. I've been able to do this many times, and it is always a lot of fun.

## A few things to consider when you're planning a creative retreat for you and your friends:

**First, the retreat does not have to be an entire afternoon.** Two to three hours is actually the perfect amount of time. Most people don't have hours and hours of free time anyway, so setting parameters in the beginning is to your advantage.

**There are two different kinds of creative afternoons.** One, you all bring your own projects and spend a couple hours working on them while catching up on all the latest news. Two, one of you teaches the rest a skill, and you learn a new craft or project together.

> Everyone brings his or her own stuff, so you don't have to worry about making sure you have enough supplies to go around.

The advantage of the first option is the cost for supplies is free. Everyone brings his or her own stuff, so you don't have to worry about making sure you have enough supplies to go around.

However, it's also fun to try new things, and if your friends are up for it, you can ask that they all pitch in some money for supplies.

If you or a friend are teaching a craft, have the supplies ready beforehand and ask your teacher friend to arrive an hour early to set up. It always takes longer than you would think to do simple things. If all the supplies are prepped, you can easily get into the learning part after everyone arrives.

**You don't have to go overboard on snacks and drinks.** I usually serve fresh fruit, some sort of drink, water, and a treat. Usually everyone is so busy working on their projects they hardly eat anything anyway, so don't kill yourself making macaroons (unless you love making macaroons—then go for it).

**Send out an email invitation** to let your friends know ahead of time about the creative retreat. When the day comes, have FUN!

## Rachel Anne Ridge

Mom, Nana, Writer, and Artist
http://rachelanneridge.com
http://homesanctuary.com



**Describe your business or mission.** I encourage people to find the beauty in their lives through my writing and art.

**What does a creative retreat look like for you?** Finding personal creative time is a challenge! My job has been creating art for the past fifteen years, so I'm constantly doing art for others… not necessarily for myself. In order to find personal time, I feel like I have to finish all my household chores—which of course, are never done! It has helped me to have my own creative space— a corner of the house that is all for my mess. It is out of the way so no one can see it. That way I don't have to clean up, and I'm more likely to do things as I'm able.

**How do retreats benefit you?** Every time I spend any amount of time away from my home office, I come back with new ideas for creating. I've never taken a specific "creative" retreat, but just stepping away from my everyday life, even for a weekend with my family, gives me a chance to see things in a new light. As a creative, I need to see new things and experience them with my senses in order to stay fresh.

**Any advice for someone who is just starting out with taking personal retreats?** I'd say that there is never a "good" time to step away from your everyday responsibilities. There will always be a reason to put off taking a personal retreat, not least of which is that you'll feel that you don't deserve it. But if you are serious about creating, I think you owe it to yourself to invest the time to find out what makes you tick, what inspires you, and how you can express yourself best through your art. It takes time and patience to find your creative voice, and retreats can be a way to jump-start the process as well as build on what you've already started.

# The Secret Power of Little Things

Most of us don't get too excited about the little things. Grocery shopping, laundry, explaining "why" for the hundredth time to a toddler—those things don't seem to carry purpose in them.

But something I've been learning this year is that the little things make a life. Purchasing and preparing food brings nourishment to our bodies, cleaning creates a peaceful place to dwell, and answering those questions stretches our own thought processes while building a relationship.

Derek Sivers echoes this thought in his book*:

> "If you think your life's purpose needs to hit you like a lightning bolt, you'll overlook the little day-to-day things that fascinate you."

These "day-to-day" things are worth exploring. Especially since they're your life. How many artists have taken those little things and made them seem extraordinary? We get that chance every day.

* "Anything You Want" —Derek Sivers

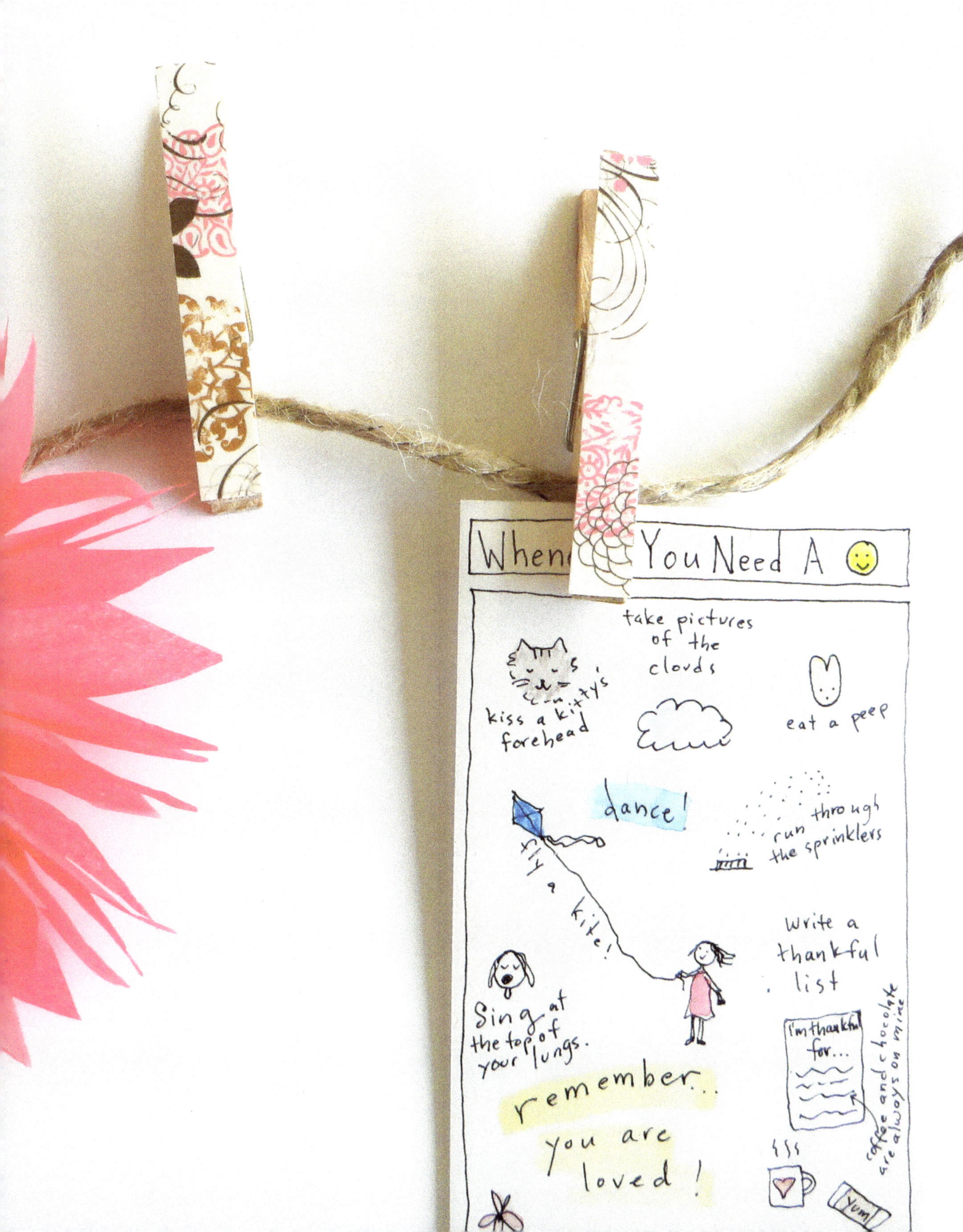

When You Need A :)
take pictures of the clouds
kiss a kitty's forehead
eat a peep
dance!
run through the sprinklers
fly a kite!
write a thankful list
Sing at the top of your lungs.
I'm thankful for...
coffee and chocolate are always on mine
remember... you are loved!
Yum

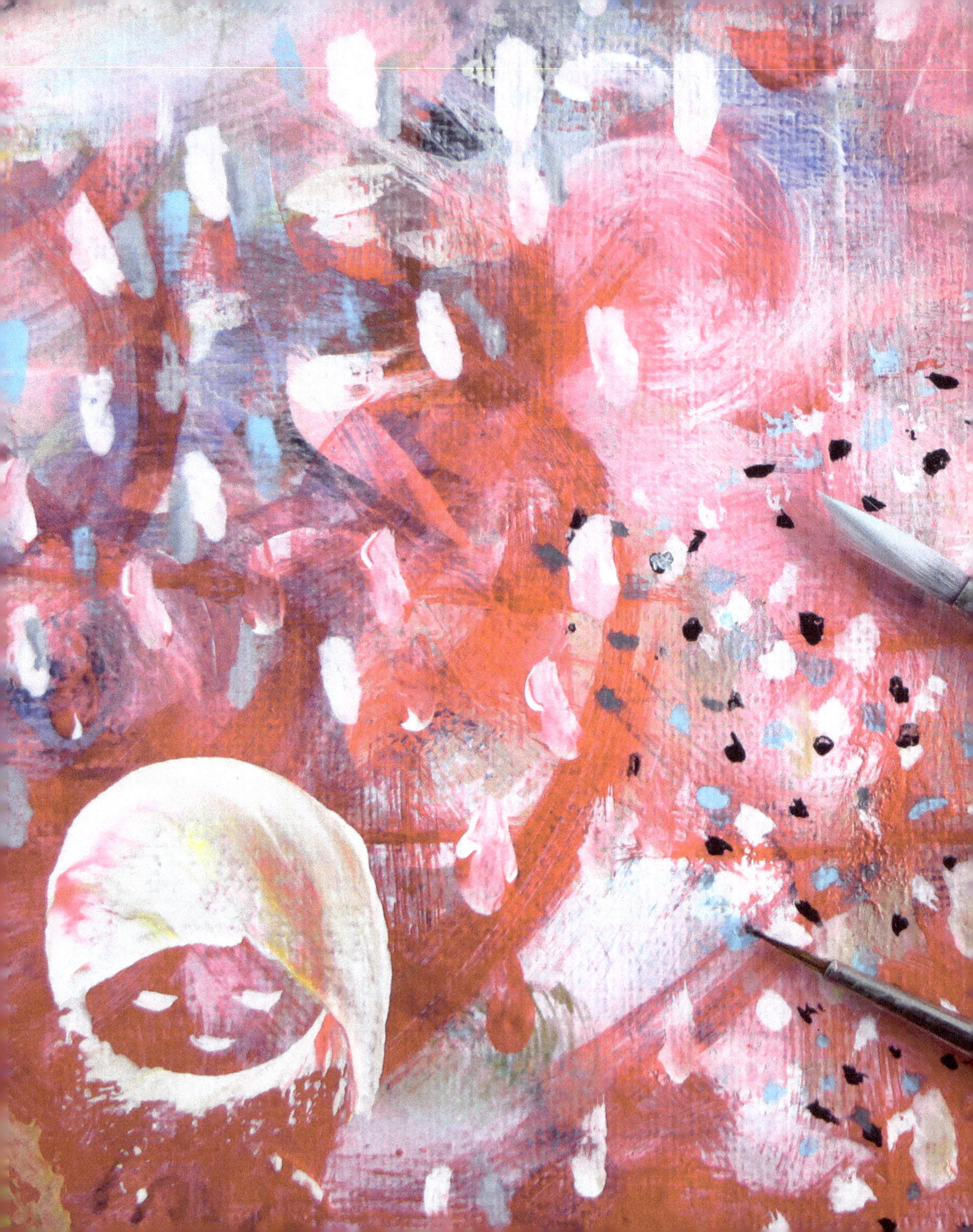

## Maggie Groover

Maggie's Butterfly Kisses
http://maggiesbutterflykisses.blogspot.com

> "A creative retreat for me looks like a break from the stress of everyday life to create something with my hands, even if only for five minutes."

**Describe your business or mission.** I am a high school student looking forward to the future. I have a passion for creativity and making the most of the resources I have been given. My mission is to inspire individuals, artists or not, to expand and explore their creative potential (and get excited about it) in a way that glorifies the Creator.

**What does a creative retreat look like for you?** A creative retreat for me looks like a break from the stress of everyday life to create something with my hands, even if only for five minutes. It could be something as small as painting a watercolor scrap to incorporate on a card later. It is crafting for the joy of it—engaging the mind while relieving it at the same time.

**How do retreats benefit you?** I don't have a business yet, but retreats do benefit my blogging. When I take a break from all this blogging knowledge (which is very good in moderation) to really let my brain rest, it can be so rejuvenating, allowing new ideas and possibilities to bloom and grow! Retreats benefit my personal life in a much deeper way, I think. This question was hard for me to answer because taking retreats is such a normal and everyday part of my life. I don't think of all those little crafting breaks I take throughout the day as retreats. It's a lifestyle for me. All I can say is, both from a business and a personal point of view, that I can't imagine life without them. Barely a day goes by that I don't craft with my hands in some way.

**Any advice for someone who is just starting out with taking personal retreats?** Don't stress it. Just pick up a pen and a piece of paper and go! Doodle, scribble, copy a verse. Don't try to make a masterpiece. Oftentimes something truly beautiful happens when you're not trying very hard.

# NEVER, EVER STOP MAKING STUFF.

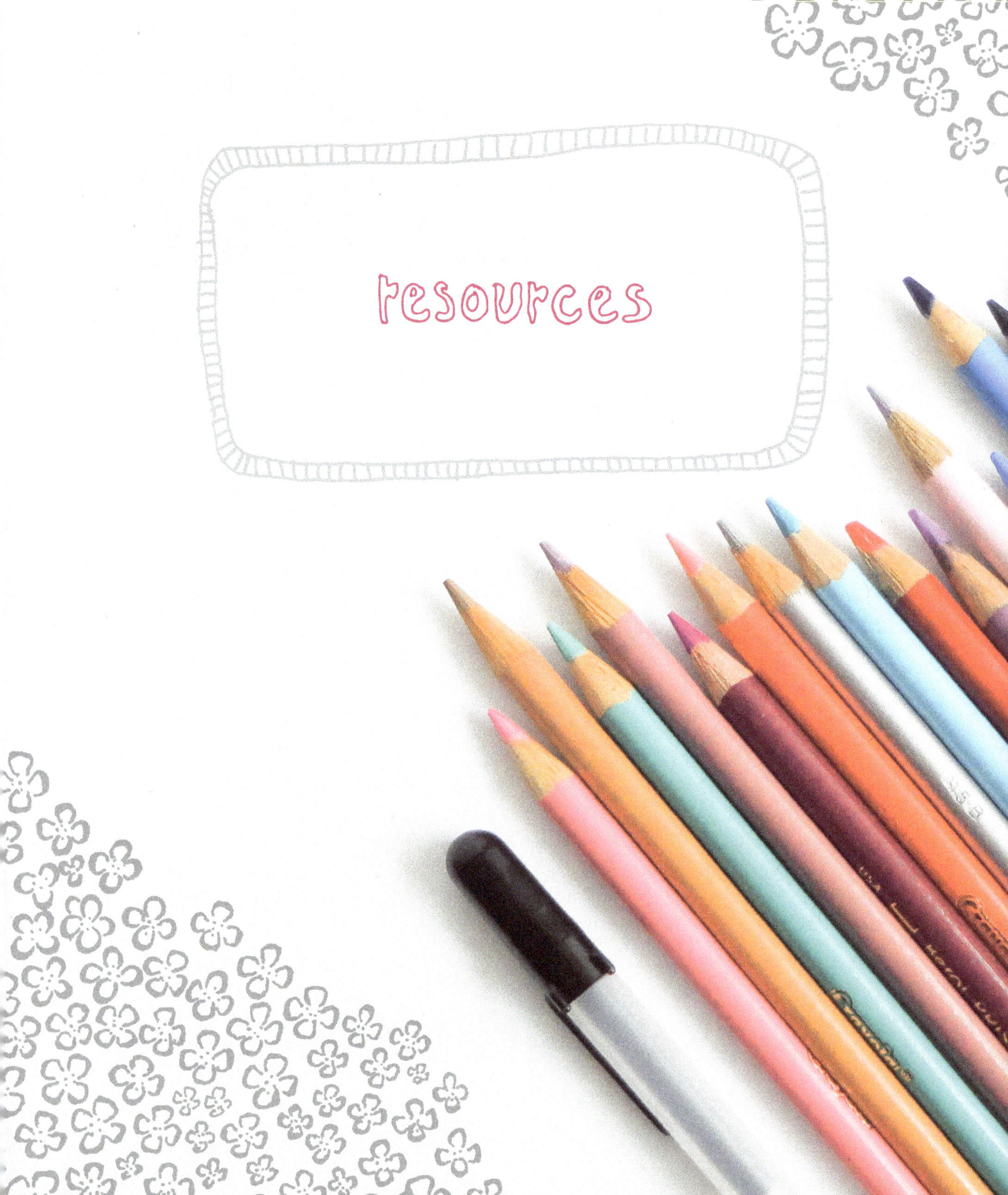
resources

Is a retreat a retreat if there is no treat involved? This is a question that I don't even want to know the answer to. On the next page is my go-to chocolate chip cookie recipe for retreat time. I don't make them every week, but they are perfect when you don't want a huge batch of cookies but need something sweet to go along with your coffee.

In this section there is also a page where you can place sticky notes of your to-do list since I always think of a million things I need to be doing the second I sit down. I've also included a page of encouragement cards with some fun creativity quotes as well as a page of blank affirmation cards for you to fill out. Write your favorite verses, lyrics, or quotes onto them for those times when you need an extra dose of encouragement.

You might find yourself wanting to jot some ideas down as you're enjoying your retreat, so there are several journal pages in this section as well. I like to write quotes out from the books I'm reading so I can reference them later; you might want to write a list of the books you want to read this year. Your choice!

And I couldn't resist adding some coloring pages in just because. Have fun!

*have fun*

## Mini-Batch Chocolate Chip Cookies

4 tbs butter

⅓ cup sugar

¼ cup brown sugar

1 egg

¼ tsp vanilla

¾ cup flour

¾ cup old-fashioned oats

¼ tsp salt

¼ tsp baking soda

⅛–¼ tsp cinnamon

¼ cup semi-sweet chocolate chips

Preheat oven to 350°F.

In a medium bowl, cream together the butter with the sugars. Add the egg and vanilla and beat until smooth. In a separate bowl, mix the flour, oats, salt, baking soda, and cinnamon together. Pour into the sugar mixture and mix until combined. Add the chocolate chips and mix.

Drop teaspoonfuls onto a cookie sheet and bake 10–12 minutes.

Makes one dozen cookies.

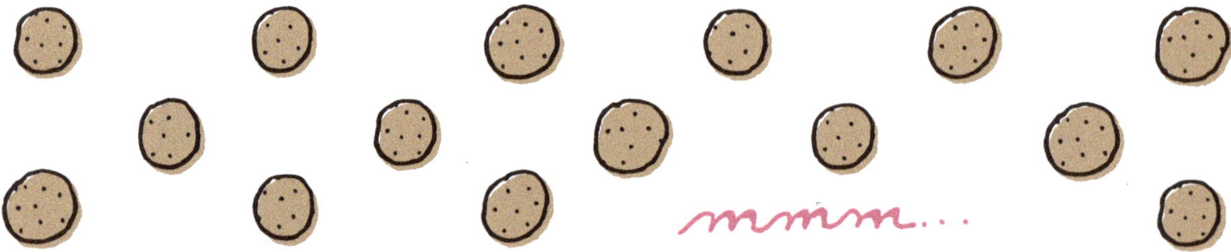

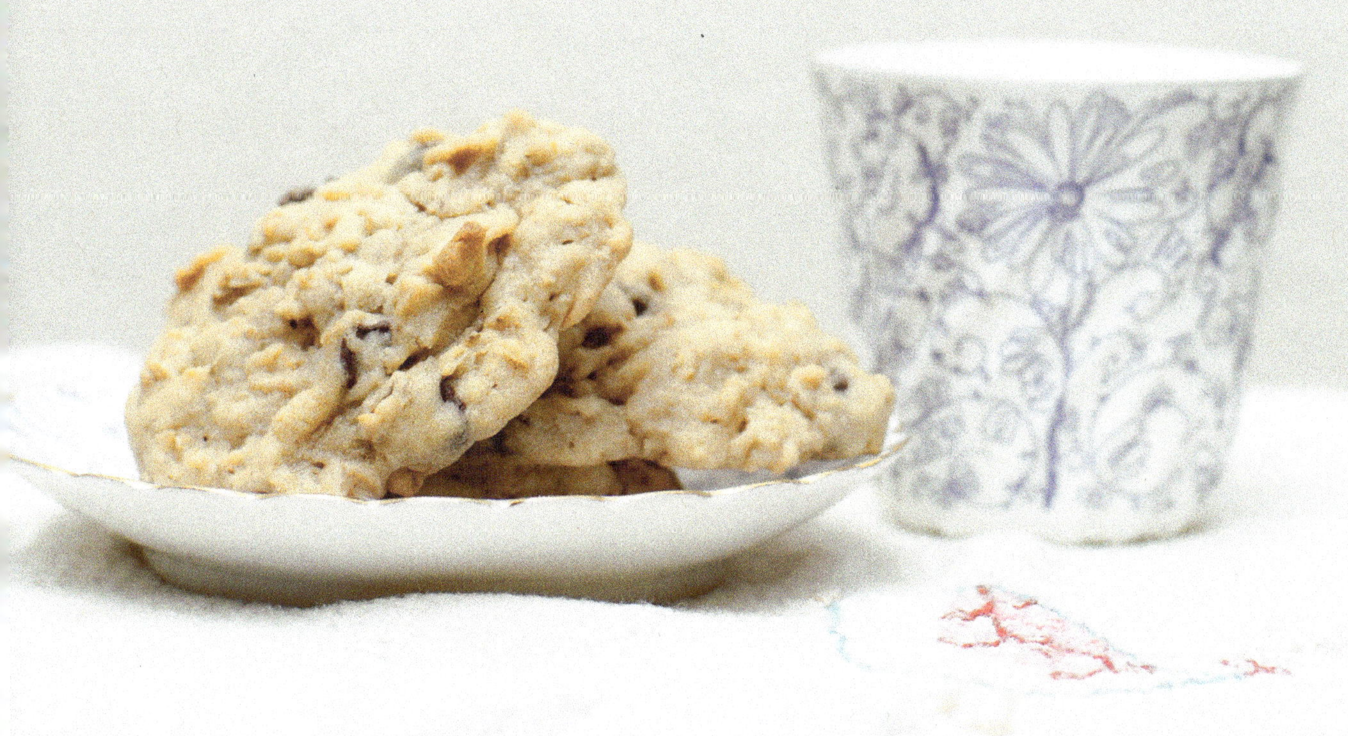

YOU CAN'T USE UP creativity.
THE MORE YOU USE,
THE MORE YOU HAVE.
— MAYA ANGELOU

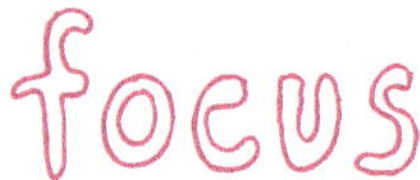

## Things I need to do when
## I get home.

The second I sit down for a retreat, I inevitably remember 800 things I need to do when I get home. Rather than letting those items distract me, I've created this page that I can turn to, quickly jot down a few reminders, and get back to my retreat's purpose.

I recommend adding a sticky note to each square on this page to write on. The nice thing about using this method is you can peel the note off and stick it in your planner after you're home from your retreat. (And this page can be reused over and over!)

## Abby Lawson

Just a Girl and Her Blog
http://justagirlandherblog.com



**Describe your business or mission.** I strive to create a beautiful, thriving home, life, and business and help others to do the same.

**What does a creative retreat look like for you?** Occasionally I am able to escape to a hotel by myself for a weekend while Donnie watches the boys. I typically spend my time writing, creating printables, and recording video for projects we have in the works. I know that is a mix of work and play, but it is fun for me and feels great to have a chunk of my project out of the way!

**How do retreats benefit you?** I stress less about completing my projects because I can get a big part of them out of the way from the get-go. I also have time to re-energize since I am an introvert and get energy from being alone. :)

**Any advice for someone who is just starting out with taking personal retreats?** Don't feel guilty about taking time for you. You'll feel better about yourself and your life, and that will project on everyone around you!

I'M CREATIVE,
YOU'RE CREATIVE,
WE'RE ALL CREATIVE.

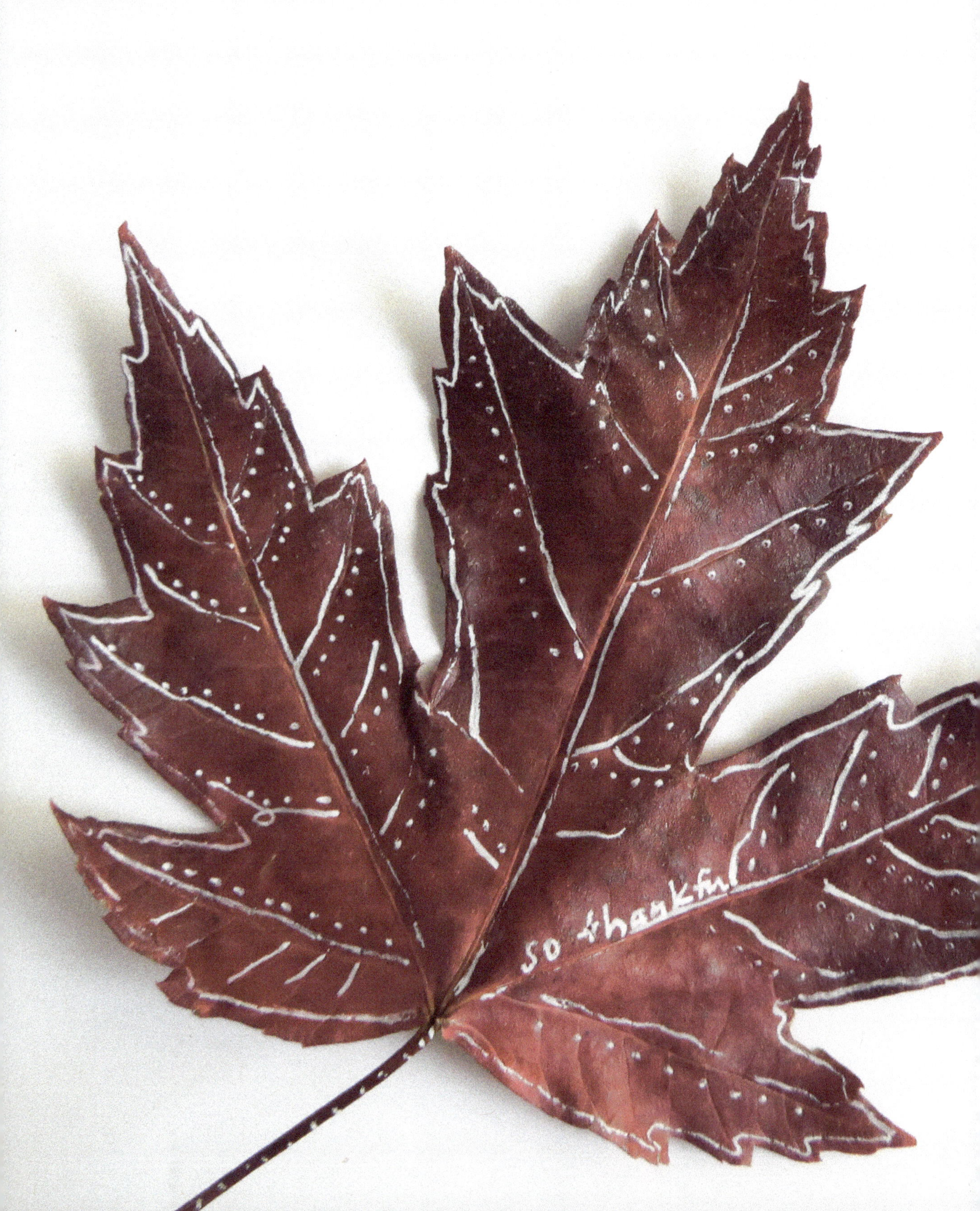

so thankful

GO AHEAD *make something*

CREATIVITY TAKES *courage*

CREATIVITY *loves a challenge*

CREATIVITY IS *contagious*

LOOK FOR *beauty*

WHEREVER YOU ARE *be all there*

Affirmation Cards — Write your own affirmations in the spaces below.

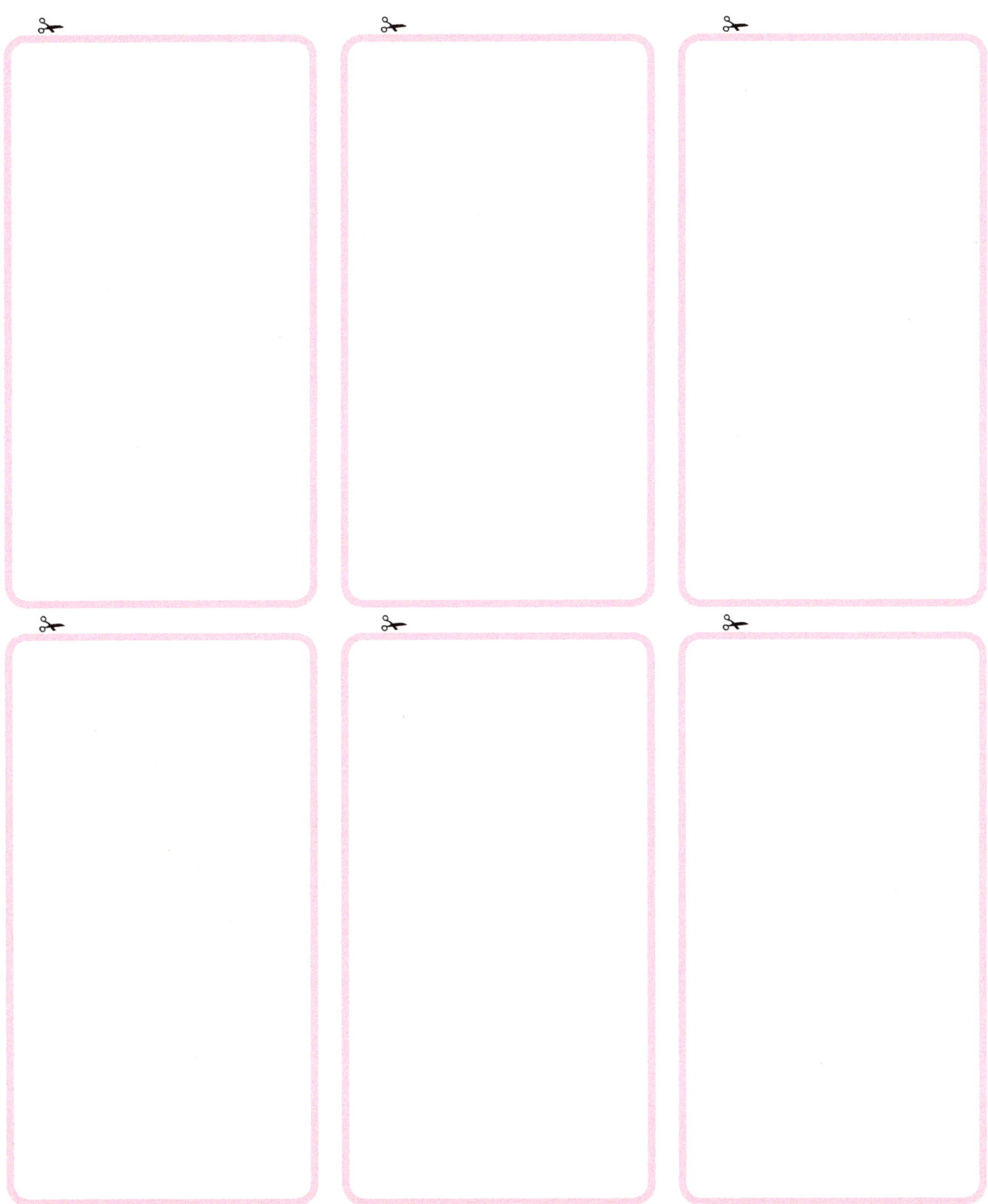

# Emily Kennedy

Two Purple Couches
http://twopurplecouches.com



**Describe your business or mission.** I am a writer, blogger, and maker. Two Purple Couches is the place where I share my crafting, DIY, and homemaking adventures. I am on a mission to craft a colorful home, one DIY at a time.

**What does a creative retreat look like for you?** There are a couple of different retreats that I like to take. The first one is more of a "make" retreat. For me, this looks like setting aside some time (could be an hour, could be a whole afternoon) to create—to paint, draw, letter, or sew. Whatever it is, it will involve getting hands-on and creating something. The other type of retreat I enjoy is a writing retreat, and for this especially, I prefer to get out of the house and work in a cafe or coffee shop for a few hours. During my writing retreats, I might brainstorm ideas for my blog, or I might write something more reflective and introspective. Ideally, I get to do both of these types of retreats each week. I try to choose a day or time and write it on my calendar so that I make sure to keep this time for myself.

**How do retreats benefit you?** The more time I give myself to create and to write, the better I feel, and the more creative I feel. It's sort of like practicing a musical instrument or sport—the more time you dedicate to it, the better you become. Retreats give me the opportunity to get ideas out of my head and into a more real and physical space. They help me recharge, experiment, and stretch outside of my usual routine. I can always tell when I've gone too long without a retreat— it's almost like I go through withdrawal! I get antsy and impatient, even cranky!

**Any advice for someone who is just starting out with taking personal retreats?** My first retreat was finally sitting down to learn how to paint with watercolors—something I'd been wanting to try for years but kept putting off for various reasons and self-doubts. It felt so indulgent, even a little selfish, to pencil in an afternoon for playing with watercolors. But hours later, after I'd gotten absorbed into what I was learning and creating, I couldn't believe I'd put it off for so long. I was so excited about this new medium to explore and so proud of my budding new painting skills. I just needed this first retreat to prove to myself how worthwhile and beneficial it was to take this time for myself. Do not feel guilty about taking a personal retreat! We all need time to recharge in some way—don't cheat yourself out of it!

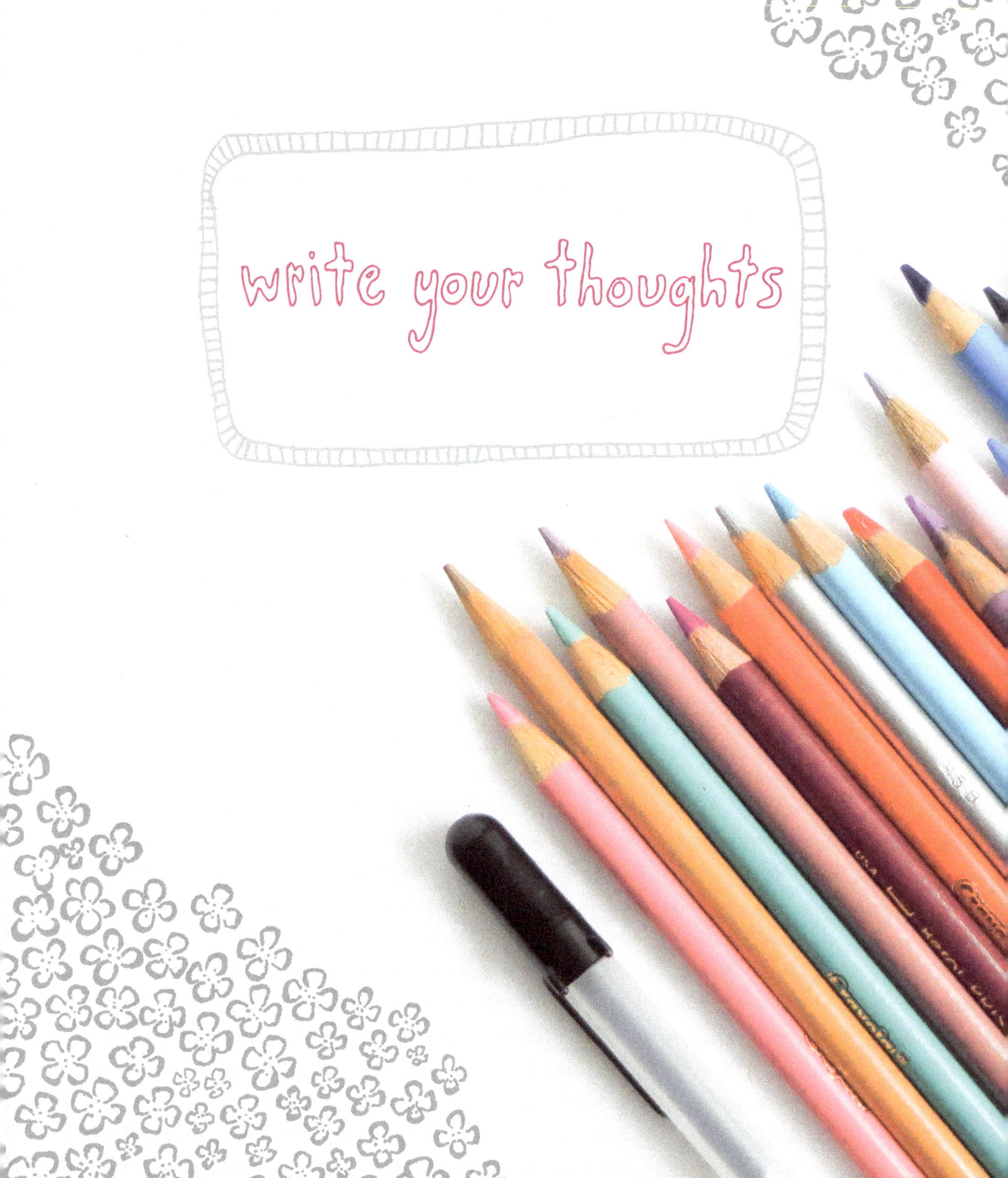


write your thoughts

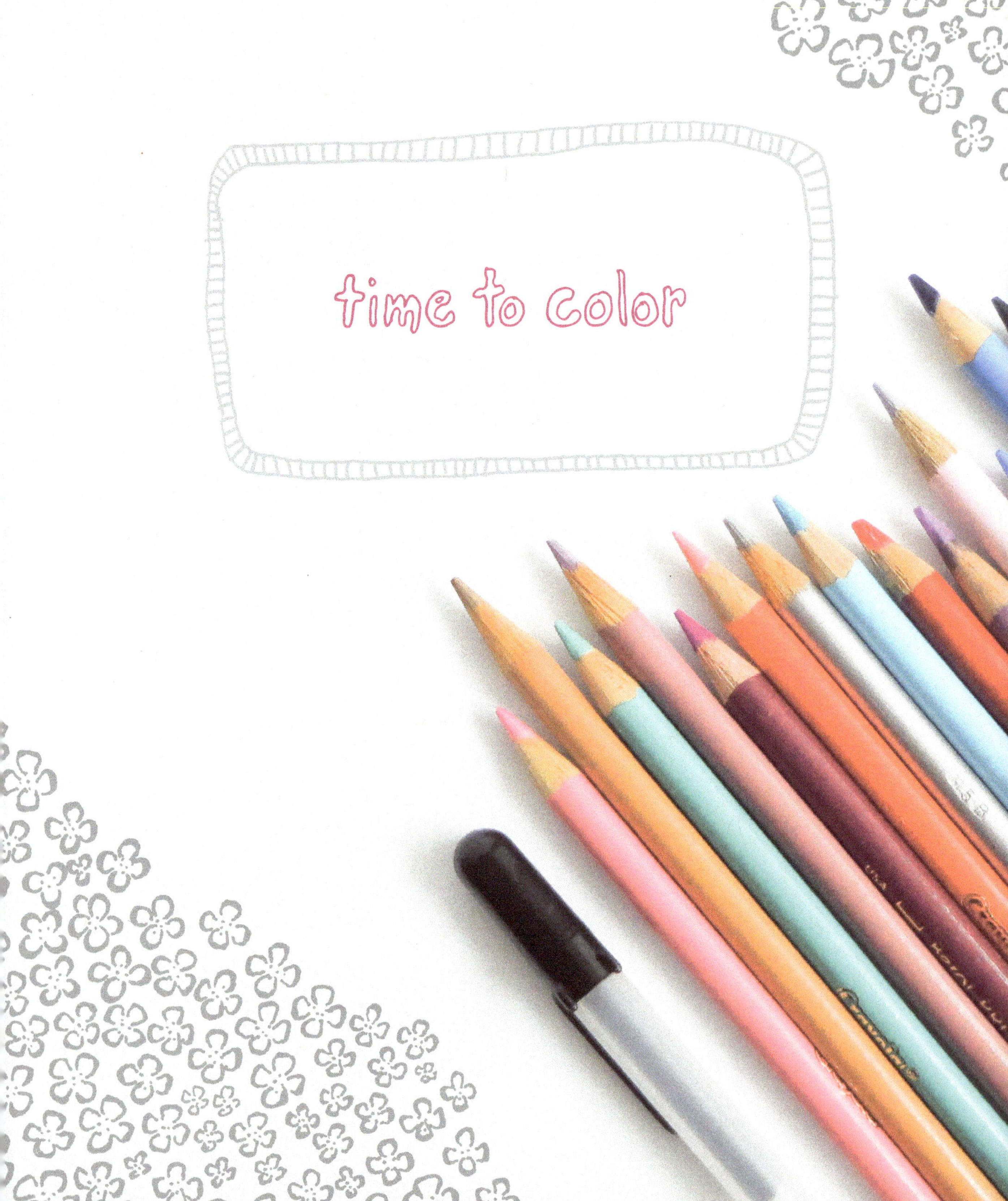

time to color

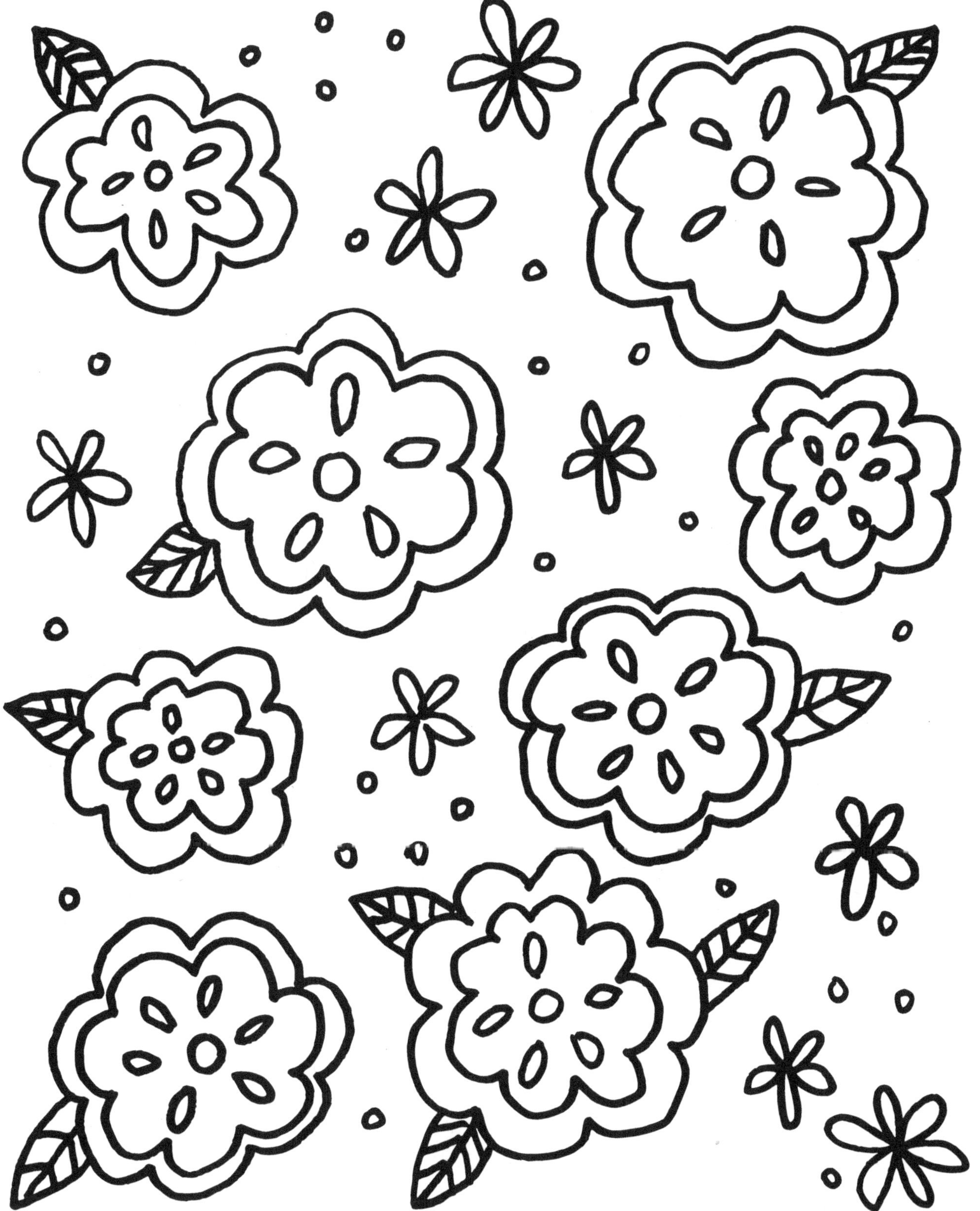

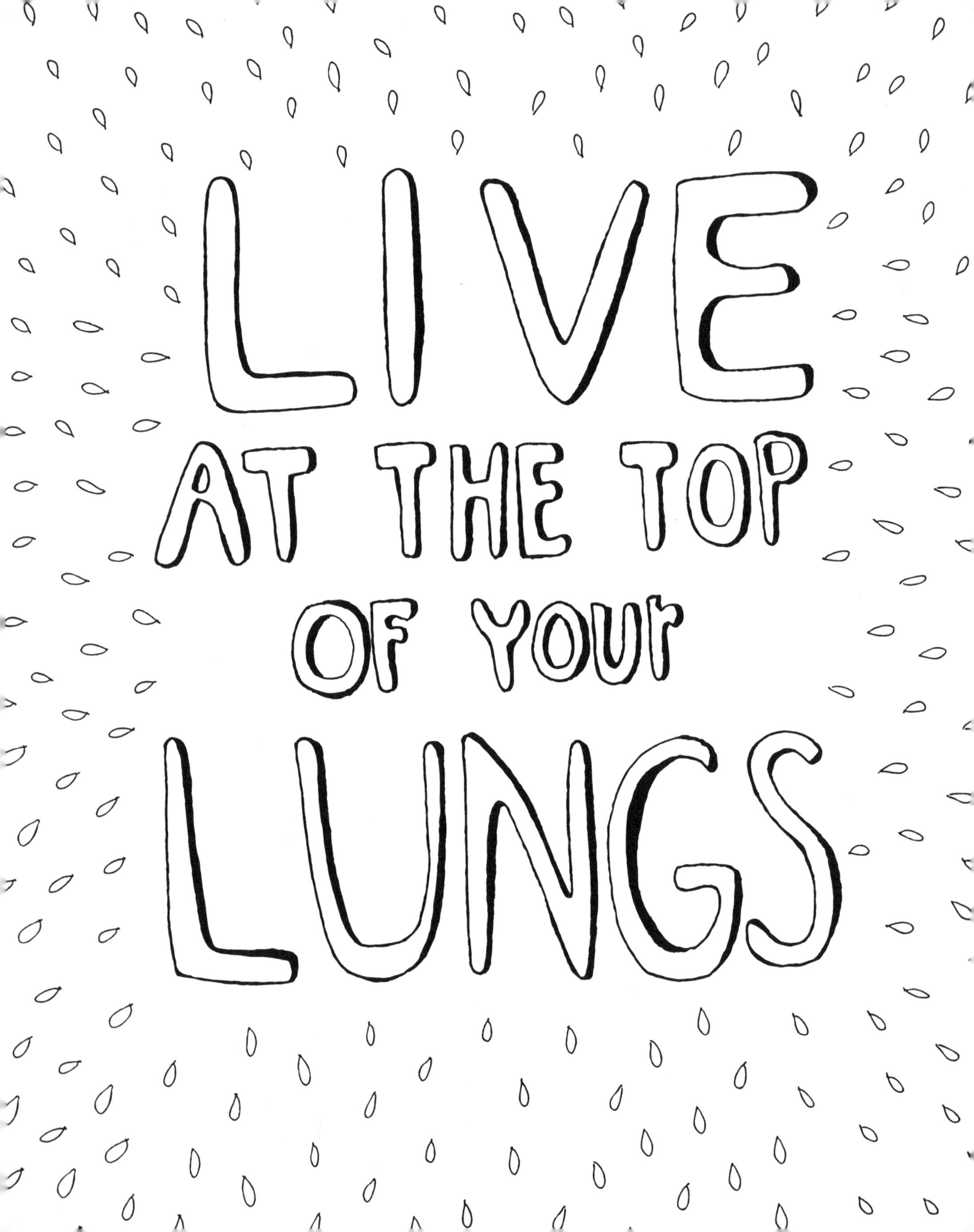

LIVE
AT THE TOP
OF YOUr
LUNGS

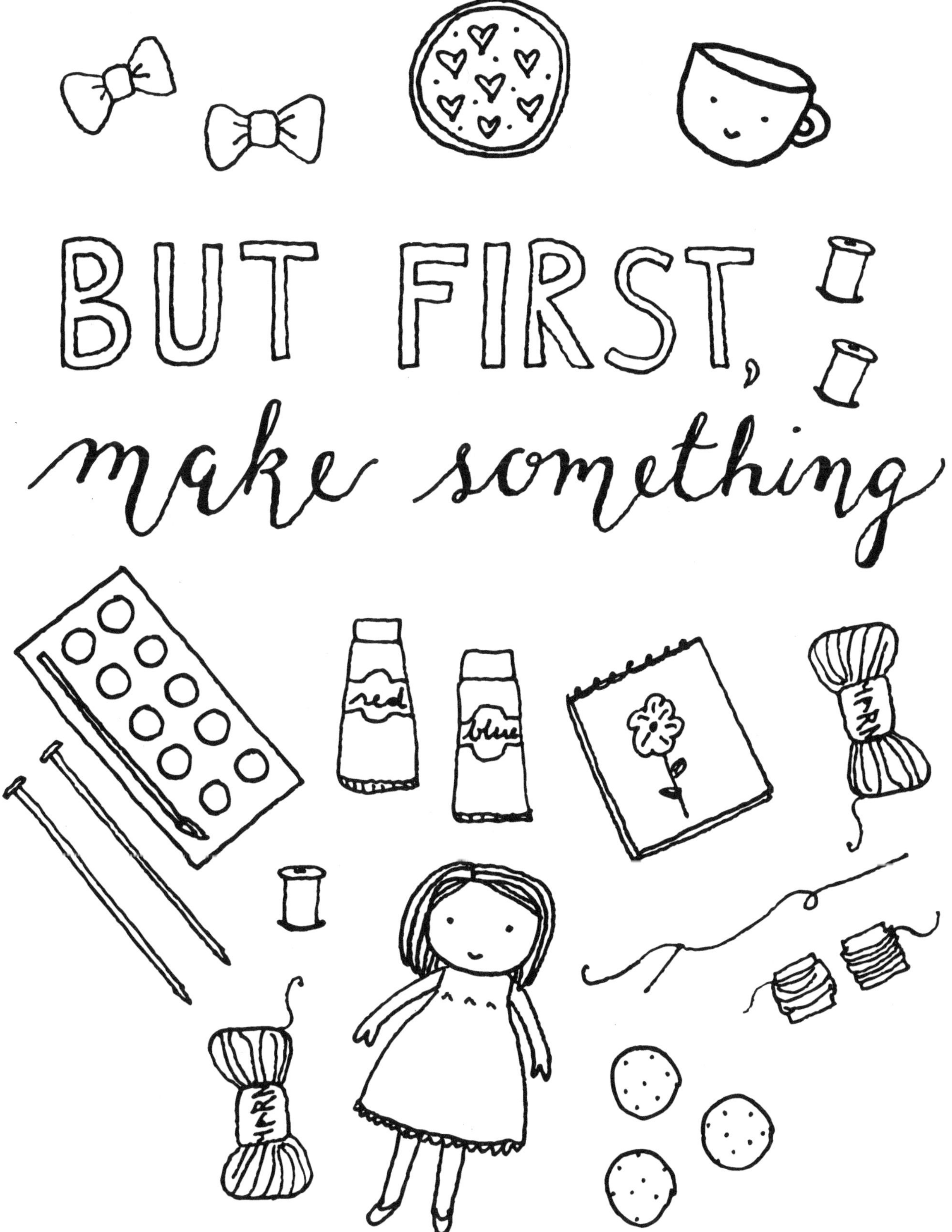

BUT FIRST,
make something
red
blue

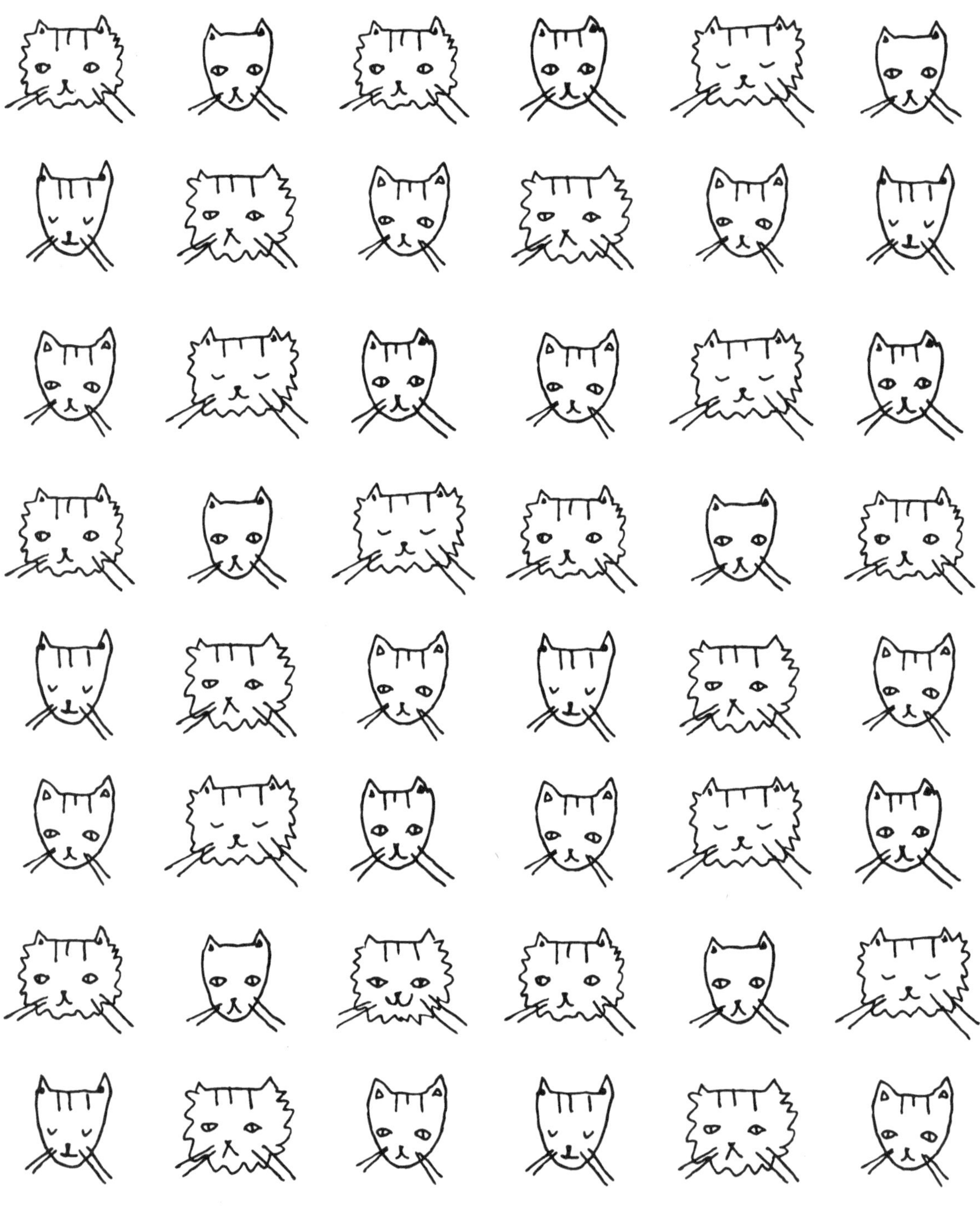

find the happy cat

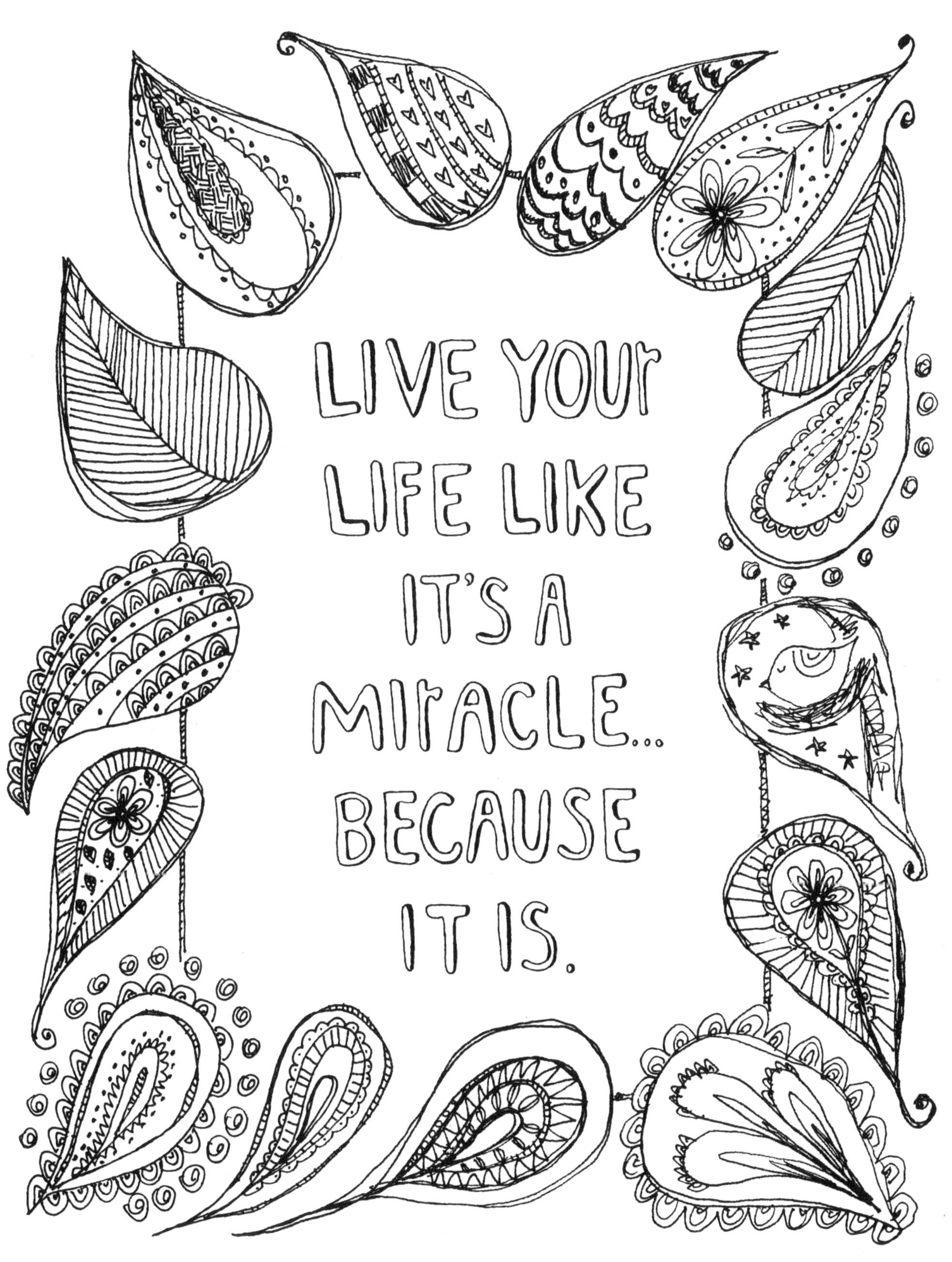

LIVE YOUR
LIFE LIKE
IT'S A
MIRACLE...
BECAUSE
IT IS.

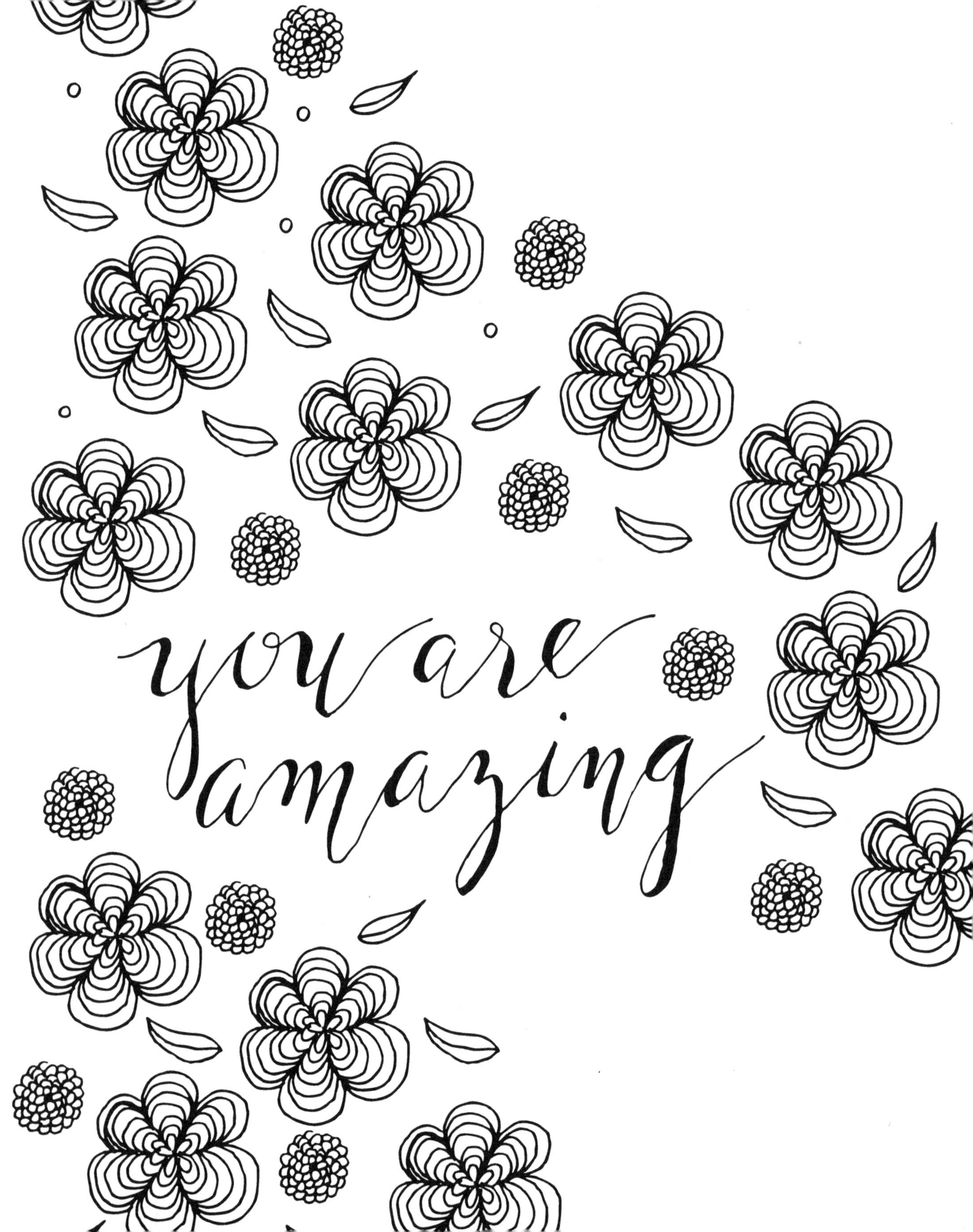
you are
amazing

WHO ELSE CAN BE WONDERFUL, BEAUTIFUL YOU?

# What others are saying

*"As a busy work-at-home mom who encourages other writers, I was always disappointed that I never had enough time for my own creative writing projects. Jennie's suggestions in* The Creative Retreat Workbook *gave me tons of practical ways to make creativity a priority in my full schedule!"*
**Ashley Brooks**
Brooks Editorial

*"After scribbling and doodling my way through* The Creative Retreat Workbook, *I am convinced that mini-retreats are not only something I need in my busy life but something I now have the tools to make happen. Jennie truly has a gift for helping readers overcome their fears in order to unlock their creative potential."*
**Lauren Lanker**
The Thinking Closet

*"Retreats are honestly how I keep my sanity and creativity flowing. They are so necessary, and this thorough, fun, and beautiful guide and workbook is the perfect way to plan something amazing for yourself. I love all of Jennie's unique ideas. Get this, and do this!"*
**Regina Anaejionu**
byRegina.com

*"Jennie's workbook is just what I've been needing! My creative to-do list is always growing, but I rarely set aside time for myself to actually create anything. Throughout these pages, Jennie provides a perfect balance of inspiration, encouragement, and structure to give me that push I need to dedicate time to my creative pursuits."*
**Emily Kennedy**
Two Purple Couches

*"Finding quiet time to plan for my blog and set creative goals is something I've struggled with but I've always wanted to do. I never really knew where to get started. The tips and practical applications in* The Creative Retreat Workbook *are just what I needed! I feel encouraged and excited to take creative retreats to focus my time, even if it's only an hour or two. I also have a creative calendar started for the first time ever (crazy right?), and I'm excited to keep it going. Thanks Jennie for all the info, worksheets, and activities you put together to make this so fun and easy to do!"*
**Beverly McCullough**
Flamingo Toes

*"I have been truly inspired by Jennie's crafting of* The Creative Retreat Workbook! *This amazing resource will help you be intentional about taking creative time for you! Filled with encouragement and equipping you with tips to get organized,* The Creative Retreat Workbook *is a must-have resource!"*
**Cathy McInnes**
Three Kids and a Fish

*"*The Creative Retreat Workbook *is the perfect tool to walk you through crafting your own personal retreat. The workbook is full of ideas and suggestions but gives you plenty of space to record your own thoughts and goals as well. The cute illustrations, beautiful photographs, and quotes throughout will be sure to inspire you on your own personal retreat!"*
**Sarah Korhnak and Beth Anne Schwamberger**
Brilliant Business Moms

9 780692 713600